THE EASY
CHRISTMAS COOKIE
COOKBOOK

THE EASY
CHRISTMAS COOKIE COOKBOOK

60+ RECIPES TO BAKE FOR THE HOLIDAYS

CARROLL PELLEGRINELLI

Photography by Hélène Dujardin

ROCKRIDGE
PRESS

For general information on our other products and services or to obtain technical support, please contact our Customer Care Department within the United States at (866) 744-2665, or outside the United States at (510) 253-0500.

Rockridge Press publishes its books in a variety of electronic and print formats. Some content that appears in print may not be available in electronic books, and vice versa.

Interior and Cover Designer: Lisa Forde
Art Producer: Karen Williams
Editor: Pam Kingsley

Photography by Hélène Dujardin © 2020,
Food styling by Anna Hampton.
Author photo © Debbie McFarland,
The Studio at Daisy Hills Farm.

ISBN: Print 978-1-64739-722-7
eBook 978-1-64739-426-4
R0

**I DEDICATE THIS BOOK
TO MY MOTHER, MARIANNE.**
*She was the one who fueled my passion for baking
Christmas cookies. Mother,
not a day goes by that I don't think of you.*

Contents

Introduction

BOTH OF MY PARENTS WERE GOOD COOKS AND BAKERS, but when it came to baking cookies, my mother was the best. Oh, how I miss those days of coming home from school to the smell of freshly baked cookies. I'd spend the rest of the day up to my eyeballs in sprinkles and sweet icing. Baking Christmas cookies was even more fun as there were more types of cookies available for decorating and munching on. I can still see lots of red and green sugar everywhere. Heaps of white coconut were like mountains of snow that were surrounded by rivers of melted chocolate for dipping. Scents of cinnamon, vanilla, and citrus filled our home. I remember the very best cookies were always the warm ones I sneaked off of the cooling racks.

All of these Christmas cookie memories and more can be yours, too. Recipes are handed down from one generation to the next, and many a family tradition is formed around making them. It's a wonderful way to honor your roots, especially during the holidays.

If you don't have any special recipe traditions, adopt one by choosing a cookie from this book to get started. Baking Christmas cookies is the perfect family activity. There is something for everyone to do—from making the dough to decorating the finished product. More meaningful memories will be formed making cookies than watching a movie together. Having a large group of people to your house for the Christmas holidays? Wouldn't it be nice to have a variety of cookies to offer them? One sure way to get different cookies without having to bake them all yourself is to hold a cookie swap—one of easiest parties you'll ever host.

Use this book to learn the basics of making cookies and to inspire new Christmas cookie traditions. Try new recipes and don't be afraid to try new methods. Once you master cookies, you can get the hang of any type of baking. Make every day Christmas by making your own homemade Christmas cookies any day of the year.

CHAPTER ONE

The Christmas Cookie Handbook

In this chapter, you'll find everything you need to know about making Christmas cookies. Once you've absorbed this information, you're ready to tackle any of the recipes found in these pages. Start out with how to read a recipe and how to measure the ingredients. Learn about the different ways of combining ingredients and what to do once they are combined. Baking, cooling, and cookie storage are also covered. You'll find plenty of ideas for decorating your Christmas cookies that go way beyond colored sugar and sprinkles. Learn about icing, piping, painting, and more. Use the ingredient list as a guide to stock your pantry so you can get baking whenever you wish, and use the equipment list to take a baking inventory. You'll also discover steps for hosting a cookie swap, creative ways to display your cookies, and tips for giving cookies as gifts.

Holiday Prep: Sugar, Butter, and Sprinkles

Making cookies is a snap—if you're prepared to do it. Being prepared is the one sure way to make your Christmas cookie baking experience a success. The first step is to familiarize yourself with the recipe. What ingredients and equipment are needed? How much time will it take to bake the cookies? What type of cookies are they, and what methods are used to make them? Once you've gathered the ingredients, how are they measured? Different ingredients require different measurement techniques. Learn everything you need to know, and before long, it will be second nature. Baking cookies, especially Christmas cookies, should be fun!

Read the Recipe

You'll find that all of the recipes in this cookbook are formatted in a similar manner, but other recipes and other cookbooks may be laid out differently. That's why it is important to carefully read a recipe before you begin. To make sure I have all of the necessary ingredients, I read over a recipe several times before making it. Someone may have used all of the eggs to make breakfast that morning. Was that baking *soda* or baking *powder*? I also do it to visualize myself making the recipe. This helps to ensure I have the necessary equipment, too. Besides looking at the ingredients and equipment, make sure to note the timing. A cookie may bake in 30 minutes, but the beginning of the recipe may say the dough should be made the day before.

Recipe Measurements 101

To get the best-tasting and best-looking cookies, you must properly measure the ingredients. A friend shared that a batch of cookies she baked did not rise at all. She said the last time she had made them, all she could taste was the baking soda, so she left it out. We looked at her recipe together and discovered that she thought the recipe was calling for 2 tablespoons of baking soda when only 2 teaspoons were needed!

Dry Ingredients

Flour, confectioners' sugar, brown sugar, granulated sugar, baking soda, baking powder, salt, and spices are most of the dry ingredients found in a cookie recipe. They should be measured using dry measuring cups and spoons (see Tools and Equipment, page 14).

Flour and confectioners' sugar are measured in the same manner. As they are light and airy, they need to be handled gently and not scooped out of the container with a measuring cup. To retain their airiness, use a teaspoon to fill the measuring cup over the brim. Using the flat edge of the spoon handle, cut across the top of the measuring cup, allowing the excess flour or confectioners' sugar to fall back into its container.

Even though brown sugar has a moist texture, it needs to be packed into a dry measuring cup. Spoon the brown sugar into the measuring cup, using the spoon to press down after each addition. The measurement is complete when the brown sugar is flat and even with the rim of the cup.

Granulated sugar can be scooped out of its container with a dry measuring cup until the cup is full and the top is level. The other dry ingredients are measured with measuring spoons. Scoop the dry ingredient with the measuring spoon and level off the top.

Wet Ingredients

Wet ingredients include water, milk, and oil. These are measured in a "wet" measuring cup made of clear glass or plastic. Hold the cup at eye level to make sure the amount you add is correct. It may look like the right amount if you're looking down on it, but there may not be enough. Flavored extracts can be measured using measuring spoons. One of my favorite finds is a liquid measurer that looks like a shot glass; I find it much easier to use than measuring spoons. The side of the glass has measurements in teaspoons, tablespoons, ounces, and milliliters. The most it holds is 2 tablespoons.

Weight versus Volume

In baking above all other cooking, it's important that the ingredients are measured as specified in the recipe. If amounts are not precise, your cookies won't rise or they may taste "off." When flour is measured in a dry measuring cup, you're actually measuring the volume of the flour, not the weight. One cup of all-purpose flour weighs 4½ ounces or 120 grams. The recipes in this book are all written according to the US system of measuring volume, not weight. If ingredients are measured as instructed previously in this section, your cookies will come out great. Most European cookbooks use the metric system, with measurements in weight. The United Kingdom uses both the imperial system and the metric system. It's important to note that imperial and US system conversions are different. One quart in the US system equals 16 ounces as opposed to 20 ounces in the imperial system. There is a chart located in the back of the book to help with any necessary conversions (see page 145).

Techniques

Here are techniques that apply to baking cookies, including ones that may not be used in other types of cooking. They are simple to remember. Once you master them, there won't be a cookie recipe out there that you'll be afraid to make. Baking Christmas cookies will be a snap.

Mixing

A recipe is made of up various ingredients, and those ingredients typically have to be mixed together. It isn't any different when making cookies. For a successful cookie, you must start with a properly combined dough. That said, I remember reading a cookbook where the chef threw everything into her stand mixer bowl, covered the machine with a kitchen towel, and turned it on high. To this day, I'm still afraid to try that method.

SIFTING

In older recipes, almost all of the dry ingredients were sifted together prior to adding them to the bowl. These days, flours and ingredients such as baking powder are a finer quality and less lumpy, so sifting isn't necessary. To make sure my dry ingredients are well mixed, I use a wire whisk. The only item that still needs to be sifted is confectioners' sugar, which contains lumps. You don't want a lump to stop you from squeezing out icing onto a cookie. To sift confectioners' sugar, measure it out into a wire mesh strainer over a large bowl. Gently shake the strainer and the sugar will fall into the bowl. Eventually all that will be left are the lumps, which can be broken up or thrown away.

CREAMING

Nearly all cookie recipes instruct you to cream your butter and sugar. You need room-temperature butter for this to work. Mix the butter first to make sure it's soft enough before adding the sugar. Next, add the sugar to the bowl. Using an electric mixer, mix until the butter and sugar are well combined. Scrape the sides of the bowl down as you go.

FOLDING

This is a term that is used when stiffly beaten egg whites or whipped cream are added to another mixture prior to baking. To keep the air that is captured (the volume) in the egg whites or whipped cream, the ingredient is stirred in a spoonful at a time in a figure-eight motion using a spoon or silicone spatula. Once it's folded in, you may still see a bit of the egg whites or cream and that's okay.

JUST COMBINED AND HAND-STIRRED IN

Both of these refer to when ingredients are incorporated but still can be seen in the mixture. This technique is used, for example, when add-ins are mixed into cookie dough just before shaping. Ingredients like dried fruits, chocolate chips, and nuts should be hand-stirred in. You wouldn't want them pulverized by the mixer.

COMPLETELY COMBINED

When ingredients are completely combined, they are mixed so well that they appear as one mass. You won't see a patch of flour or any egg yolks.

Chilling

Unless you have a very cold kitchen, you may want to chill your cookie dough after all of the ingredients are combined prior to baking. Using chilled cookie dough is the key to not having it spread too much during baking. For example, to chill sugar cookie dough, remove it from the bowl and form it into a flat oval. Completely wrap the dough in plastic wrap. Place it on a plate and put it in the refrigerator. I will even put my mixing bowl in the refrigerator in between baking batches of drop cookies.

Rolling and Cutting

To prepare for making sugar cookies, I get out my bread board. It is fine to use your kitchen counter as long as it's cleaned with dish soap, not a harsh spray. Put some flour in a small, shallow bowl and sprinkle a small amount of that flour on your work surface. Use your hand to spread the flour evenly over the surface. Next, dump your cookie dough out on to the board. With floured hands, flatten it out into an oval. Sprinkle a little flour over the oval. After lightly flouring your rolling pin, it's time to roll out the dough. Begin from the middle of the dough and roll outward. Each time the rolling pin is lifted, start back in the middle and roll to the edges. This will keep the edges from getting too thin.

Once the dough is ¼ to ⅛ inch thick, it's time to cut out the cookies. Dip the cookie cutter into the shallow bowl of flour before pushing it down into the cookie dough. Be sure not to twist or move the cookie cutter around when it's in the dough. Just pull it straight up after cutting. Depending on your dough, you may wish to cut all of the cookies out first and then put them on the prepared baking sheet, or you may transfer them one at a time.

Decorating

Decorating cookies is one of the best activities for all ages. It's perfect as a family effort, and it makes a fun school activity, too. Adults and older children can make the cookie dough and roll it out. Children ages 7 and older can use cookie cutters to cut out the cookies. Adults and older children under adult supervision can bake them. Once the cookies are cooled, everyone can get into the action with decorating.

FROSTING AND ICING

The terms *frosting* and *icing* are used interchangeably. Both are used to describe the actual sugar concoction and how it is applied to cookies, cakes, and more. Some say that *frosting* refers to a thicker mixture and *icing* is thinner and shiny. Buttercream is my favorite frosting. It can be simply made with butter, sugar, and a little milk to thin it out. Flavoring, such as vanilla extract, is also incorporated. Add Dutch cocoa and you have chocolate frosting. Quite often buttercream frosting is made with solid shortening instead of butter. Shortening helps the frosting keep its shape and last longer, but the flavor isn't as good. For intricate cookie decorating, a thin icing, like royal icing, is used. Royal icing is made with water instead of butter.

Her Majesty, Royal Icing

Royal icing is to cookies as fondant is to cakes. They are both excellent to decorate with and are more about looks than about flavor. You can make royal icing with pasteurized egg whites, but I prefer using meringue powder. The consistency of the icing is controlled by how much water is used. To color royal icing, simply add food coloring a few drops at a time until the desired hue is achieved. The same goes for gel food color, only you'll need much less. Keep in mind that once the icing dries, the color will be darker.

4 cups confectioners' sugar	5 tablespoons warm water	3 tablespoons meringue powder (see Resources, page 146)

Carefully measure the confectioners' sugar 1 cup at a time by using the tea-spoon method (see Dry Ingredients, page 2), and sift it using a mesh strainer over a large bowl. Add the warm water and the meringue powder. Using an electric mixer, beat on high speed until stiff peaks form, about 10 minutes. If you have a stand mixer, mix on low speed for the same amount of time. This makes a stiff icing. For a medium-consistency icing, add ⅛ teaspoon of warm water for every cup of stiff icing. Fold in the water with a silicone spatula. For flooding, or covering a cookie completely, use a thin icing. To get a thin-consistency icing, add ½ teaspoon of warm water for every cup of stiff icing. Don't incorporate it too quickly; instead, use a figure-eight motion to mix in the water.

PIPING

If you want to up your game, you'll want to go beyond spreading the icing with a knife. Instead, use a piping bag and piping tips to decorate your cookies. Piping bags, couplers, and tips can be easily purchased online or in local craft stores. Traditional cloth bags and store-bought plastic icing bags are not strictly necessary; icing can be piped from a resealable plastic bag.

To fill and use a piping bag:

1. Place an icing tip coupler in the corner of the bag. Cut a hole in the corner of the bag just large enough for the end of the coupler to fit through. Place the desired icing tip onto the coupler. Secure the icing tip onto the coupler with the coupler ring.

2. With one hand, grab the middle of the bag with the open end up. Use the other hand to fold the sides down over the hand holding the bag. Next, place the bag, tip down, into a tall glass for stabilization.

3. Use a silicone spatula to transfer icing to the bag. Once the bag is halfway to two-thirds full, unfold the sides and tightly twist the open end several times. Make sure there are no air bubbles in the icing and that it goes down into the tip.

4. You'll need both hands to pipe icing onto your cookies. One hand will twist and push the icing out of the tip and the other hand will be the guide.

PAINTING

Painting cookies is simple and fun to do. All you need is some type of food coloring, food-safe paintbrushes, and something to put the "paints" in. The day before painting, bake and ice your cookies. This allows the icing to set completely. To use gel food coloring to make paints, use ½ teaspoon of gel food coloring for every 1 teaspoon of water. You can also use regular food coloring and mix it with flavor extracts if you choose. Food coloring is added by drops. Begin with 3 or 4 drops and go from there. Once the paint dries, the color will become darker. I have a dozen glass soufflé cups to hold various colors. If desired, add sprinkles and other nonpareils while the paint is still wet.

Sprinkles, jimmies, colored sugars, sanding sugars, French dragées, Red Hots, and other shapes are known as *nonpareils*. Nonpareils come in endless colors and children of all ages love to decorate with them. Using these are the easiest way to decorate Christmas cookies. Most of the nonpareils can be put on the cookie dough either before baking or after baking when there's wet icing or food paint to hold them on. One of the prettiest ways to use them is after piping or painting a design on a cookie. Take the cookie and dip it upside down into a plate of sprinkles. After a few minutes, it'll be ready to eat.

3 Easy Steps for Flooding

Have you ever seen a cookie that is decorated in such a way that the icing is perfectly even and shiny? It almost seems as if it is floating on top. That icing method is called "flooding." Here is how you do it:

1. With stiff icing (the consistency of toothpaste), pipe an outline of the area to be filled.
2. Pipe thin icing into the outlined area. Depending on the look you desire, it can be the same color as the outline or a different color.
3. Smooth out and remove bubbles from the thin icing either by using a tool, such as a toothpick, or by shaking the cookie back and forth.

Storage and Freezing

The Christmas holidays can be very stressful. To save myself added stress, I like to make several batches of cookie dough ahead of time and freeze it for baking later. How the dough is frozen depends on the type of cookie. For example, I will freeze a drop cookie, such as Classic Chocolate Chip Cookies (page 59), as measured balls of dough. I place them on a baking sheet and freeze them overnight. The next day, I transfer them from the baking sheet to resealable plastic bags, which I then put in a plastic container to go back in the freezer. They can be baked one at a time while still frozen. Dough for Christmas Sugar Cookies (page 29) or other roll-out cookie dough can be frozen in batches, then thawed and rolled out later. The cookie dough will maintain its flavor for up to 3 months. With a little advance preparation, I can serve a variety of cookies in under 30 minutes.

Already baked cookies can be frozen, too. Carefully place them in an airtight container with parchment paper between each layer. If they are decorated, they need to be completely dry before freezing. Place each decorated cookie in its own plastic bag. Next, carefully place them in a hard-sided plastic container so they don't get damaged. These need to defrost completely on the kitchen counter while still wrapped.

Frozen frostings and icings will keep their flavor for up to 3 months. Defrost them completely before using them. Both cookie dough and icing can be stored safely in airtight containers or bags in the refrigerator for up to 4 days.

For day-to-day storage, keep soft cookies in airtight containers. Decorated cookies are also stored in airtight containers, but try to avoid stacking them. Crispy cookies should be stored in a loose-lidded container, like a cookie jar.

Building a Cookie Board

A cookie board is one way to display several types of cookies for a party or other event. Before putting cookies on the board, place bowls of dipping chocolate, colorful icing, or even crushed pieces of candy each with a small spoon so guests can top their cookies with goodies. Group the cookies on the board according to size or type. When you have only a few different types to display, divide the batches in half and separate the halves. Got open spaces? Place fancy wrapped candies, candy canes, or other eye-catching edibles in between the cookies. Expecting a larger crowd? Decorate a tabletop or buffet with cookies. Put down a tablecloth first. Use doilies on good china plates. Display cookies on cake stands and other holders with different levels. Place holiday-themed items in between the plates or stands, such as pretty glass ornaments or sprigs of fresh evergreen.

The Christmas Baker's Kitchen

There is nothing more frustrating than to be in a cookie-baking mood only to find that a run to the store is required. Christmastime is busy enough. Alleviate some of the stress by being prepared to bake. One way is to stock your pantry ahead of time. Use the following list to shop for the key ingredients found in most Christmas cookie recipes. Of course, some of the optional items may be needed, as well. Besides these ingredients, it's also important to have the right baking equipment; some tools are absolutely necessary, while others are merely nice to have. Of course, the oven is the most important piece of baking equipment. How well do you know yours?

Staple Ingredients to Stock

If you keep these ingredients on hand, you'll be able to bake cookies anytime you wish.

All-purpose flour: If the recipe says just "flour," this is the flour to use. There are other flours, such as bread, whole-wheat, self-rising, and almond flours. Unless specified in the recipe, these flours may adversely affect the baking results.

Baking soda: Also known as sodium bicarbonate, this leavening agent makes cookies rise. The majority of cookie recipes call for baking soda.

Baking powder: Like baking soda, baking powder makes cookies rise. In fact, most baking powders are made with baking soda, cream of tartar, and cornstarch. Some recipes use baking powder alone, but many use it along with baking soda for an extra leavening boost.

Cream of tartar: This ingredient is found in most vintage cookie recipes. Cream of tartar is used to help activate the rising process in baking soda. It is not usually seen in modern recipes that call for baking powder, which contains both baking soda and cream of tartar. Cream of tartar is sometimes used to stabilize egg whites, especially when making meringues. Several recipes in this book call for this ingredient.

Salt: It's difficult to find many cookie recipes that don't call for salt, which is a flavor enhancer. Cookies made without any salt or salted butter will taste flat. For the recipes in this book, you can use regular table salt.

Butter: All of the recipes in this book call for salted butter. I have at least 4 pounds of butter in my refrigerator at all times. If I have more than 4 pounds of butter on hand, the extra is stored in the freezer. Butter can be frozen for up to 3 months while still maintaining its full flavor.

The Better Butter

There are so many butters on the market, but which one makes the best cookie? My rule of thumb is to save the very best butters for spreading on bread. I use moderately priced butter for cookie doughs, and I don't use inexpensive butter at all for baking. I admit that the only time I will not follow a cookie recipe exactly is when it calls for unsalted butter. I can't tell you how many times I've taken a bite out of a perfectly beautiful cookie only to be underwhelmed by the flavor. The reason is that the baker used unsalted butter. Some say unsalted butter is fresher, but I get better results with salted butter, which is what all the recipes in this book call for. I keep it on hand specifically for baking. If you prefer to use unsalted butter or it's all you have, simply add ¼ teaspoon of salt per each 8 tablespoons of butter in the recipe, but the flavors will meld better when you use salted butter.

Vegetable shortening: These days, most people prefer using butter to shortening, but shortening does have its advantages: It has a much longer shelf life than butter. Cookie doughs made with shortening are sturdier and will hold their shape longer. Vegetable shortening is also less expensive.

Vegetable oil: This type of oil is occasionally used in making cookies. While olive oil may be substituted, its specific flavor may not work for the cookies you're making. Flavorless refined coconut oil is another option, but it is difficult to work with as it's a cross between an oil and a solid shortening and needs to be melted before using.

Eggs: Large is the standard egg size. Very few cookies are made without eggs. Eggs not only help bind the ingredients, but they also add volume if well beaten.

Sugar: The most common form of sugar used in making Christmas cookies is granulated sugar. When you see "sugar" in the ingredient list for a recipe in this book, use granulated sugar.

Light brown sugar: A larger-grained sugar mixed with molasses, light brown sugar is used in many drop-cookie recipes. Dark brown sugar has more molasses in it and may affect the cookie flavor.

Confectioners' sugar: Also known as powdered sugar, icing sugar, or XXX/10X sugar, confectioners' sugar is another must-stock ingredient that typically is used by itself on the surface of the cookie or is a component of the frosting. It is a sugar that is ground very fine (10X is the finest grind and 3X the least fine) and is powdery in texture. Confectioners' sugar always has cornstarch in it to make it even lighter. If you prefer not to use confectioners' sugar made with cornstarch, you may grind your own granulated sugar in the food processor.

Unsweetened cocoa powder: Dutch-process cocoa powder is darker and less acidic than natural unsweetened cocoa powder—the latter is typically what I have on hand. I've never noticed any more acidity, because my recipes typically already include baking soda and/or baking powder, which naturally neutralizes acidity.

Vanilla extract: Especially in the United States, vanilla extract is found in most baked goods. The more expensive the vanilla, the more robust the flavor.

Spices: The most common spices used in Christmas cookies are cinnamon and nutmeg. I also always keep ground ginger, cardamom, and cloves in my pantry.

Food coloring: If colored icing is used frequently, then icing gels are most desired as they offer more vibrant colors. Icing gels need a more practiced hand as they can be very tricky to work with. Also, too much gel will impart a bitter flavor. Standard food coloring from the grocery store works fine for occasional use. It's hard to go wrong with food coloring.

Optional Ingredients to Stock

You may also want to include the following special ingredients in your pantry:

- Semisweet chocolate chips and other forms of chocolate

- Candy-coated chocolates and other candies

- Sanding and sparkling decorative sugars, such as colored sugars

- Nonpareils, such as sprinkles, themed sprinkles, chocolate jimmies, French dragèes, Red Hots, and sugar pearls

- Additional extract flavors, such as almond, orange, lemon, cinnamon, anise, and rum

- Other spices, such as ground cloves, allspice, ginger, cardamom, anise, and mace

- Nuts, such as pecans, walnuts, or almonds—nuts can last for months in the freezer

Tools and Equipment

To make the baking process easier, you need to get acquainted with some specific kitchen tools.

MUST-HAVE

Here are the kitchen tools that are essential for making the Christmas cookies in this book.

Electric mixer: Cookie dough can be mixed by hand with a wooden spoon—but it will take a lot of strength, especially for a heavy cookie, like a drop cookie. Electric mixers come in a large price range. Buy what you can afford, but if there is a choice, choose one with the strongest motor.

Baking sheets: You'll need two of these. They come in all sizes and materials. I prefer the 13-by-18-inch shiny metal pans with 1¼-inch sides. They are also known as "half sheet pans." The shiny metal ensures even baking. The sides allow for the pan to be used for other things, like bar cookies and roll cakes. Two are needed to either bake at the same time or rotate with another batch.

Cooling racks: Two of these are ideal. Most cookies need to cool a bit first on the baking sheet while sitting on a cooling rack. Then the cookies need to be transferred from the pan to the rack for complete cooling.

Mixing bowls: You'll need at least two or three of these, including one large bowl. Ceramic and glass mixing bowls are popular, but I prefer my stainless steel bowls because they are lightweight and unbreakable.

Wet and dry measuring cups and spoons: Wet measuring cups come in various sizes, from 1 cup to 2 quarts. The 2-cup measuring cup and the 4-cup (1-quart) glass ones get the most use in my kitchen. A full set each of dry measuring cups and measuring spoons is necessary. Dry measuring cups come in 1-cup, ¾-cup, ½-cup, and ¼-cup sizes. Measuring spoons are usually attached; a basic set comes in 1-tablespoon, 1-teaspoon, ½-teaspoon and ¼-teaspoon sizes.

Wire mesh strainer: In these recipes, a wire mesh strainer is used exclusively to sift confectioners' sugar.

Wire whisk: This tool is used to thoroughly mix dry ingredients.

Silicone spatula: This is good for scraping down the sides of a bowl and for spreading things like melted chocolate.

Metal spatula: Use a metal spatula to remove cookies from the baking sheets.

Cooking spray, parchment paper, or silicone baking mat: Any one of these will work to keep your cookies from sticking to the baking sheets. I vary which one I use depending on the cookie I'm baking.

Rolling pin: A regular wooden rolling pin with two handles works just fine, but there are other types available, as well. I own several rolling pins. The one I got from my grandmother is a hollow ceramic type with a cork in each end. You fill the inside with cold water. It works best for pie pastries. My wooden French rolling pin has tapered ends, which makes it easier to roll dough flat-handed. I also have a stainless steel rolling pin similar to the French one. The metal stays cooler while rolling. Which one do I use the most? A regular wooden rolling pin with two handles.

Cookie cutters: A huge set of cookie cutters isn't necessary; just choose the shapes you prefer. They come in almost every shape you can imagine. There are even companies that will make one just for you. I prefer metal cookie cutters, but plastic ones work, too.

Give Your Oven Some Lovin'

The oven is the most important piece of equipment for any cookie baker. How well do you know your oven? Do you have a convection oven setting? If so, you can bake at 25°F lower than a recipe specifies, and your cookies will finish 25 percent faster. Are your cookies getting burnt? Check the temperature calibration with an oven thermometer. Is one side of the pan cooking faster than the other? Make sure it isn't touching another baking sheet or the walls or door of the oven. Are you using dark cookie pans? If so, lower the oven temperature by 25°F from what the recipe instructs. This may also lengthen the baking time. Baking at a high altitude makes a big difference in cakes but not as much in cookies. Be sure to set a timer, but always use your nose as a backup. When I begin to smell the cookies, they usually are done or are very close to being done, no matter the time.

NICE TO HAVE

This baking equipment isn't totally necessary for making cookies. It will just make the process even simpler.

Stand mixer: I can't lie; this is my favorite cookie-making tool. Making cookie dough is a breeze with a stand mixer. You practically just throw the ingredients into the bowl and you're done before you know it. My daughter is using Ole' Bluey, the first stand mixer I had for 25 years, and I've been using Big Red, a bigger, more powerful one for the last 3 years.

Wooden bread board: I use my bread board for rolling out and cutting cookie dough. A large baking mat or a very clean kitchen countertop will work as well.

Food scale: A digital scale isn't necessary for making cookies as long as measuring cups are used correctly. But it can be a helpful tool if you want to use recipes from other countries (make sure it measures in both ounces and grams).

Professional cloth piping bags and metal piping tips: Professional piping bags and tips elevate fancy decorated sugar cookies. You can still decorate cookies by using disposable plastic bags with a small hole in the corner and a tip pushed through. Lower-priced plastic tips can be found in the grocery store baking aisle along with already-made decorators' icing. If nicer cloth bags and metal tips are preferred, most craft stores have them. Be sure to also check out yard sales and your local thrift stores.

Cookie press: Buttery cookie dough is pushed through a cookie press to form various shapes, like Christmas trees, holiday wreaths, and more.

Cookie scoops: These ensure that all of the cookies are the same size. Measuring spoons can perform the same job, just not as easily. I have a two-ended cookie scoop. One end holds 1 tablespoon of dough and the other end holds 2 tablespoons. I have to use a miniature silicone spatula to get the dough out of the scoop. There are cookie scoops that work like some ice cream scoops: You scoop up the dough and then compress the handles to flip the dough out.

Best Gift Ever

Homemade gifts are the best gifts, especially when they are edible. When deciding on edible gifts and their packaging, I'm reminded of the riddle, "Which came first: the chicken or the egg?" Sometimes, I find containers first and then I decide what to put in them. This happens when I purchase the next year's containers at after-Christmas sales. Other times, I decide on the baked goods and then have to find a container. Containers can be as simple as clear cellophane plastic bags, which can be easily found at your local craft store or online, tied with a pretty bow, or something as extravagant as a vintage cookie jar found at an antique shop.

When I am giving similar edible gifts to several people at the same time, I like to use wide-mouth canning jars. To decorate each jar, I top the lid with a square piece of Christmas fabric cut with pinking shears and attach the fabric with a rubber band. I punch a hole in a business card–size gift card I've signed and printed with, for example, "Nutty Chocolate Clusters—Made Just for You." Last, I thread the card onto a piece of coordinating ribbon and tie it around the jar, totally covering the rubber band.

About the Recipes

The recipes in this cookbook are divided into four chapters. The first recipe chapter is filled with holiday favorites. These cookies are the ones you may make or at least eat every Christmas baking season. The next chapter also features classics, but with a twist. Chapter 4 offers a few new creations that may turn into classics. The final chapter is filled with Christmas treats that aren't technically cookies, but they are featured at many cookie swaps and on cookie boards and buffets everywhere.

Be sure and look for what Louisianans call *lagniappes* ("LAN-yaps") included with each recipe. These "small gifts" come in the form of useful labels and special tips that will help ensure your cookie-baking success.

The labels you'll find throughout this book include the following:

Bar cookies: These are cookies that are baked in a rectangular or square pan and are cut into squares for serving. Some bar cookies are layered and baked a couple of times. Others are made with a single drop-cookie dough.

Contains nuts: These recipes contain nuts, such as pecans, walnuts, almonds, cashews, peanuts, and more.

Drop cookies: These are the most common type of cookies. They come in a plethora of flavors and are easily adapted to Christmas recipes.

Freezer-friendly: The texture and flavor of the baked cookie should last up to 3 months in the freezer if frozen according to the recipe instructions. Some cookie doughs can be also frozen up to 3 months.

Icebox cookies: Before the cookie dough is put into the refrigerator to chill, it is formed into a long roll. Once it is completely cold, the dough is sliced and then baked.

Molded cookies: The cookie dough is molded by hand into various shapes.

Rolled cookies: Sugar cookies are an excellent example of rolled cookies. The dough is rolled out with a rolling pin and then cut into shapes, usually with cookie cutters.

The tips you'll find throughout this book include the following:

Ingredient tip: This highlights a certain ingredient, including its unique properties or specific handling.

Serving tip: This shares ideas for how the cookies may best be displayed or served to highlight their unique features.

Storage tip: Here's where you'll find special storage instructions beyond the ones already included in the recipes, such as for freezing.

Technique tip: Other cooking and/or prepping tips will be explained here.

Traditions: This will highlight the origin of the recipe or draw attention to those with an international flavor.

Troubleshooting tip: If there is a common issue with the recipe, this explains what to look out for and how to fix it.

Variation: This will offer suggestions of other ingredients that may be used instead of the ones listed.

Host a Cookie Swap

Before your holiday calendar gets too full, be sure to choose a date to host a cookie swap. A cookie swap is one of the easiest parties to host. All you need to provide is a clean home, a big table to display the cookies, beverages, plates, napkins, and six dozen cookies for the exchange. Perhaps a couple of prizes for the contest winners, if you have a contest. A couple of weeks before the event, mail, e-mail, or message your invitations. Be sure to include all of the party details, such as in this sample invitation:

YOU'RE INVITED TO

A Christmas Holiday Cookie Swap

WHEN:
Saturday,
December 5,
at 2:00pm

WHERE:
My home

COME:
Dressed in
your finest
holiday wear

BRING: Six dozen of your decoratively displayed, tastiest homemade Christmas cookies for sharing

OPTIONAL: Bring an additional container to carry your new cookies home

INCLUDED: Hot teas, coffees, wine, and sparkling water

YOU COULD BE A WINNER IN ONE OF THESE CONTESTS: Best-Tasting Cookies, Prettiest Cookies, and Loveliest Cookie Display

PLEASE RSVP BY
Monday, November 30

CHAPTER TWO

Holiday Favorites

Everyone has a favorite holiday cookie. Mine changes from year to year. This Christmas I plan to make—and eat—lots of the tricolored Neapolitan Cookies. I really enjoy that strawberry, chocolate, and almond flavor combination. Also, the adult in me craves something that will play a little with my taste buds, like St. Nicholas Cookies (*Speculaas*), which are loaded with cinnamon, nutmeg, and cloves. But at Christmas, the person I really need to make happy is the little girl inside me. She says it's either Gingerbread People or Christmas Sugar Cookies. What's your favorite? I bet you'll find it in this chapter.

Holiday Pinwheel Cookies

Makes 28 cookies

PREP TIME: 45 minutes, plus 3 hours 20 minutes to chill | **COOK TIME:** 10 minutes

Freezer-Friendly, Icebox Cookies

You'll see many holiday pinwheel cookies out there. Two of the other popular pinwheel Christmas color schemes are red and white, and red and green. I like doing the green and white ones so that using the red sprinkles on the side stand out. Don't let the 3 hours of chilling put you off. It's very important to bake these cookies while the dough is still cold. If the dough is too warm, the rings won't bake as desired. They may run into each other, destroying the pinwheel shape you went to so much trouble to make.

2 cups flour, divided

½ teaspoon baking powder

¼ teaspoon salt

12 tablespoons salted butter, at room temperature

¾ cup sugar

1 large egg

1 teaspoon vanilla extract

1 teaspoon green food coloring

Red sprinkles

1. In a medium bowl, using a wire whisk, combine 2 cups of flour, the baking powder, and salt. Set aside. In a large bowl, cream the butter and sugar together. Mix in the egg and vanilla. Add the flour mixture, ½ cup at a time, until the mixture is well combined.

2. Divide the dough in half. Place one half on a 15-inch-long piece of parchment or wax paper. Top it with another piece of parchment or wax paper. Roll the dough between the paper pieces until it's an 8-by-12-inch rectangle. Transfer the papered dough to a baking sheet and place it in the refrigerator.

3. Add the green food coloring to the other half of the cookie dough in the bowl. Use an electric mixer to blend in the coloring. If a darker color is desired, feel free to add a little more food coloring. Mix the dough until it is completely colored.

> RECIPE CONTINUED

4. As with the first piece of dough, place the green dough in between two pieces of 15-inch-long parchment or wax paper. Roll out the dough into an 8-by-12-inch rectangle. Place it on top of the other piece of dough in the refrigerator. Chill for at least 20 minutes.

5. Remove both pieces of dough from the refrigerator. Place the noncolored dough on clean work surface. Remove the top piece of paper, being careful not to tear the dough. Remove the bottom piece of paper from the green-colored dough. Very carefully place the green dough on top of the noncolored dough by starting at an edge and gently laying the green dough down. Remove the paper from the top of the green dough. Use a knife to cut off the uneven edges.

6. Starting at one of the long sides, begin rolling up the layered doughs into a log while gently pulling the dough away from the bottom piece of paper. Once rolled, pinch the long edge to seal. Wrap the rolled dough in a piece of plastic wrap and place it back on the baking sheet and into the refrigerator. Chill for 1 hour.

7. Preheat the oven to 350°F. Line two baking sheets with parchment paper. Set aside.

8. With flat hands, gently roll the dough back and forth to get rid of any flattened surface created by sitting on the baking sheet. Chill for another hour.

9. Fill a tray with red sprinkles. Remove the dough from the plastic wrap and place it on the tray. Gently roll the dough back and forth to completely cover it with sprinkles. If needed, add sprinkles by hand to areas that didn't get covered. Rewrap the dough and place back in the refrigerator for another hour.

10. Slice off the uneven ends of the dough log. Cut the log into ¼-inch slices and place half of them 1½ inches apart on one of the prepared baking sheets. Bake for 10 minutes, until lightly browned.

11. While the first batch is baking, place the rest of the slices on the other prepared baking sheet. Place in the refrigerator until it's time to bake them.

12. Cool baked cookies for 2 minutes on the baking sheet, then transfer the cookies to a cooling rack to cool completely. Store in an airtight container at room temperature for up to 1 week.

STORAGE TIP: The plastic-wrapped rolled dough without the sprinkles will keep for up to 3 months in the freezer stored in an airtight container. Defrost in the refrigerator.

VARIATION: Make any color combination you desire. You could even divide the dough into 3 or 4 portions for more colors. Feel free to use different extracts to change the flavor.

Butter Spritz Cookies

Makes 3 dozen cookies

PREP TIME: 30 minutes | **COOK TIME:** 10 minutes

Freezer-Friendly

I remember pressing out these colorful, holiday-themed cookies with a manual cookie press, making plenty of green trees and red stars. I also remember that by the time half of the cookies were pressed, there would be butter dough all over the place. So now I cheat when I make them: I bought myself an electric cookie press (see Resources, page 146), and life got so much better.

Cooking spray

2½ cups flour

½ teaspoon salt

1 cup (2 sticks) salted butter, at room temperature

1¼ cups confectioners' sugar

2 large egg yolks

1½ teaspoons vanilla extract

Red or green food coloring (optional)

Sprinkles (optional)

1. Preheat the oven to 400°F. Very lightly coat a baking sheet with cooking spray, wiping the excess off with a paper towel. Set aside.

2. In a small bowl, using a wire whisk, combine the flour and salt. Set aside. In a larger bowl, cream the butter and confectioners' sugar together. Add the egg yolks one at a time, mixing well after each addition. Add the vanilla and mix it in completely. Mix in the food coloring (if using). If more than one color is desired, divide the dough, then add the colorings.

3. Fill a cookie press with the cookie dough. Shoot the cookies out of the press onto the prepared baking sheets at least 1½ inches apart. Scatter the sprinkles over the cookies (if using). Two baking sheets may be baked at the same time if they are placed on separate racks. Halfway through the baking process, the sheets must be switched from one rack to the other and rotated 180° for even baking.

4. Bake for 6 to 8 minutes, until the edges are brown. Cool for 2 minutes on the baking sheets, then transfer the cookies to cooling racks. Cool completely. Store the cookies in an airtight container at room temperature for up to 1 week.

TECHNIQUE TIP: Cookie presses come with a variety of disks, like trees, snowflakes, wreaths, and more. If you don't have a cookie press, use a piping bag and metal star piping tip instead. Play around with the different tips. You may not get the standard spritz cookie, but you'll at least be able to make some pretty stars.

TRADITIONS: Scandinavia, Germany, and Italy all claim these buttery Christmas cookies as their own.

Christmas Sugar Cookies

Makes 6 dozen cookies

PREP TIME: 25 minutes, plus 2 hours to chill | **COOK TIME:** 10 minutes

Freezer-Friendly, Rolled Cookies

I've been making these for as long as I can remember. My mother made them with me, and I made them with my daughter. The recipe has evolved over the years. These days, I prefer to roll out a softer, ¼-inch-thick cookie compared to when I was younger and desired a thinner, crispier cookie. I almost always freeze one-third of my dough so I can make these cookies anytime.

3¼ cups flour, plus ½ cup for dusting

2½ teaspoons baking powder

½ teaspoon salt

11 tablespoons salted butter, at room temperature

1½ cups sugar

2 large eggs

2 tablespoons milk

1 teaspoon vanilla or almond extract

Cooking spray

Corn syrup, heavy cream, or 1 egg white mixed with 1 tablespoon water (optional)

Colored sugar or sprinkles (optional)

Colored icing (optional)

1. In a medium bowl, using a wire whisk, combine 3¼ cups of flour, baking powder, and salt. Set aside. In a large bowl, cream the butter and sugar together. Add the eggs one at a time and mix. Add the milk and extract. Mix completely.

2. Shape the dough into 3 balls. Flatten the balls into ovals and wrap each in plastic wrap. Chill the dough in the refrigerator for at least 2 hours or up to 24 hours. The dough can also be frozen (see Storage tip).

3. When the dough is almost done chilling, put the remaining ½ cup of flour in a small bowl and dust your work surface and rolling pin. Pull out your favorite Christmas cookie cutters.

4. Preheat the oven to 400°F. Lightly coat two baking sheets with cooking spray. Set aside.

5. Remove 1 dough ball from the refrigerator. Roll it out to ¼-inch thickness (any thinner and your cookies will be very crispy, which may make them difficult to decorate). Dip the cookie cutter into the bowl of flour before cutting out each cookie.

> RECIPE CONTINUED

Use a metal spatula to transfer the cookies to a prepared baking sheet, leaving at least ½ inch between the cookies. Reroll the remaining dough to cut out more cookies.

6. If desired, decorate the cookies prior to baking: Paint each cookie with corn syrup (if using), then dust the cookies with colored sugar (if using). The corn syrup will help the sugar adhere to the cookies.

7. Working in batches, bake each sheet of cookies for 8 minutes, or until browned around the edges. Cool for 3 minutes on the baking sheet, then transfer the cookies to cooling racks. Repeat with the remaining 2 dough balls.

8. Once completely cooled, decorate with icing, if using. After the icing is completely set, store the decorated cookies in an airtight container between layers of parchment paper at room temperature for up to 1 week.

INGREDIENT TIP: When my daughter was in elementary school, I'd take two dozen of these to her school for decorating. I discovered that a sturdier cookie was needed for little hands. Besides rolling the dough at least ¼ inch thick, I replaced half of the butter with butter-flavored vegetable shortening. No one noticed a difference in the taste. Most importantly, the cookies didn't fall apart during decorating.

STORAGE TIP: To freeze, place the plastic-wrapped dough in an airtight container or bag for up to 3 months. Defrost in the refrigerator.

TECHNIQUE TIP: Whether you bake one or two sheets of cookies at a time is a matter of choice. If you bake two, halfway through, turn the baking sheets 180° and switch the racks they are on. I prefer to bake one sheet at a time. I don't open that door until the timer goes off or I can smell the baked cookies.

Aunt Wanda's Ginger Cookies

Makes 3 dozen cookies

PREP TIME: 30 minutes | **COOK TIME:** 15 minutes

Freezer-Friendly, Molded Cookies

Cinnamon and ginger have long been associated with the Christmas holiday season. My Aunt Wanda gave me this recipe years ago. These cookies pair beautifully with an afternoon cup of tea. The crystallized ginger is optional. I like to use it as it adds depth to the sweet-spicy ginger flavor, along with a little chewiness.

Cooking spray

2 cups flour

2 teaspoons baking soda

½ teaspoon salt

1½ teaspoons ground ginger

1 teaspoon ground cinnamon

12 tablespoons salted butter, at room temperature

1 cup sugar, plus more for rolling

1 large egg

¼ cup molasses

½ cup finely chopped crystallized ginger (optional)

STORAGE TIP: After you roll the dough into balls, you can freeze them on a baking sheet overnight, then transfer them to a zip-top freezer bag. Let them defrost before rolling them in the sugar.

1. Preheat the oven to 350°F. Lightly coat two baking sheets with cooking spray. Set aside.

2. In a medium bowl, using a wire whisk, combine the flour, baking soda, salt, ginger, and cinnamon. Set aside. In a large bowl, cream the butter and 1 cup of sugar together until light and fluffy. Add the egg and mix. Mix in the molasses. Add 1 cup of the flour mixture to the butter mixture and combine. Keep adding the flour mixture until the mixture is completely combined. Hand-stir in the crystallized ginger (if using).

3. Shape the dough into 1-inch balls. Roll the balls in more sugar. Place the dough balls on the prepared baking sheets about 1½ inches apart. Two baking sheets may be baked at the same time if they are placed on separate racks. Halfway through the baking process, the sheets must be switched from one rack to the other and rotated 180° for even baking.

4. Bake the cookies for 12 minutes or until the tops are mounded and firm. Cool for 3 minutes on the baking sheets, then transfer the cookies to cooling racks. These soft cookies can be stored for up to 1 week at room temperature in an airtight container.

Gingerbread People

Makes 2 dozen cookies

PREP TIME: 30 minutes, plus 2 hours to chill | **COOK TIME:** 10 minutes

Freezer-Friendly, Rolled Cookies

I loved decorating gingerbread men at Christmastime as a child. I also remember not liking their overly "spicy" flavor. For me, "spicy" didn't mean that the cookie was just hot to the tongue; it meant that there were way too many flavors! Of course, as an adult, I feel the more spice, the merrier. Don't be upset if your children find these cookies better for decorating than eating.

3¼ cups flour, plus ¼ cup for dusting

1 teaspoon baking soda

¾ teaspoon salt

1 tablespoon ground ginger

2 teaspoons pumpkin pie spice

12 tablespoons salted butter, at room temperature

¾ cup firmly packed light brown sugar

⅔ cup molasses

1 large egg

1 teaspoon cinnamon extract or vanilla extract

Icing, Royal Icing (page 7), and/or nonpareils, for decorating (optional)

1. In a medium bowl, using a wire whisk, combine 3¼ cups of flour, the baking soda, salt, ground ginger, and pumpkin pie spice. Set aside. In a large bowl, cream the butter and brown sugar together. Mix in the molasses, egg, and cinnamon extract. Add the flour mixture, ½ cup at a time, and combine. After the last bit of flour, combine the mixture completely.

2. Divide the dough in half and form into 2 round balls. Flatten the balls into disks and wrap them individually in plastic wrap. Chill for at least 2 hours or up to 24 hours.

3. Preheat the oven to 350°F. Line two baking sheets with parchment paper. Set aside.

4. Put the remaining ¼ cup of flour in a bowl. Flour your work surface and your rolling pin.

5. Remove 1 dough disk from the refrigerator. Roll it out to ¼ inch thick. Cut as many gingerbread people as possible, dipping the cookie cutter into the bowl of flour each time. Reroll the remaining dough to make more. Place the cookies on the prepared baking sheets. Two baking sheets may be baked at the same time if they

are placed on separate racks. Halfway through the baking process, the sheets must be switched from one rack to the other and rotated 180° for even baking.

6. Bake for 9 to 10 minutes, or until you can really smell the cookies. Cool on the baking sheets for 2 minutes, then transfer the cookies to cooling racks. Repeat with the other disk of dough.

7. Decorate the completely cooled cookies with regular icing, royal icing, or a combination of icing and nonpareils (if using). These will last for up to 1 week in an airtight container. If decorated, separate the cookies with parchment paper.

INGREDIENT TIP: Pumpkin pie spice is made with ground cinnamon, ginger, cloves, and nutmeg. If you prefer to use the separate spices, use 1 teaspoon cinnamon, ½ teaspoon nutmeg, and ¼ teaspoon cloves. Remember to check the use-by date on the spice containers. Fresh spices taste the best.

STORAGE TIP: The plastic-wrapped dough disks will keep for up to 3 months stored in an airtight container in the freezer. Defrost in the refrigerator.

TRADITIONS: The origin of gingerbread men has been credited to Queen Elizabeth I, who would present her guests with gingerbread cookies decorated in their likeness. Gingerbread houses became popular in the 1800s in Germany after the publication by the Brothers Grimm of the tale "Hansel and Gretel."

Neapolitan Cookies

Makes 32 cookies

PREP TIME: 35 minutes, plus overnight to chill | **COOK TIME:** 15 minutes

Contains Nuts, Freezer-Friendly, Icebox Cookies

As a little girl, these were one of the first Christmas cookies I learned to bake. Who wouldn't be drawn to the different colors and flavors of these cookies? And as much as I love chocolate and strawberry, my favorite layer has always been the almond-flavored one. These cookies will brighten up any Christmas cookie board or buffet. They make a good gift, too.

2½ cups flour

1½ teaspoons baking powder

½ teaspoon salt

1 cup (2 sticks) salted butter, at room temperature

1½ cups sugar

1 large egg

1 ounce unsweetened chocolate, melted and cooled

½ teaspoon strawberry or raspberry extract

6 drops red food coloring

1 teaspoon almond extract

½ cup coarsely chopped toasted almonds (optional)

Cooking spray

1. Line a 9-by-5-inch loaf pan with parchment or wax paper. Be sure the edges go over the sides. Set aside.

2. In a medium bowl, using a wire whisk, thoroughly combine the flour, baking powder, and salt. Set aside. In a large bowl, cream the butter and sugar together until light and fluffy. Add the egg and combine. Add the flour mixture ½ cup at a time. Keep mixing until the dough is completely combined.

3. Divide the dough into 3 portions. To the first portion, using an electric mixer, blend in the melted chocolate. Once the chocolate is completely incorporated, place that dough in the pan. Use your hands to press the dough down evenly in the pan. Be sure to wash the beaters in between the flavor additions.

4. To the second portion of dough, using an electric mixer, blend in the strawberry extract and red food coloring. Once the color is completely incorporated, place the dough on top of the chocolate dough. Press the strawberry dough evenly.

> RECIPE CONTINUED

5. To the final portion of dough, using an electric mixer, blend in the almond extract and the finely chopped almonds, if using. Once the almonds are incorporated, place the dough on top of the strawberry dough. Press it down evenly. Level out the top of dough as much as possible. This will be one of the edges of the cookie.

6. Place a piece of plastic wrap on the top of the dough. Wrap the entire pan in plastic wrap and place it in the refrigerator overnight or up to 24 hours.

7. Preheat the oven to 350°F. Lightly coat a baking sheet with cooking spray. Set aside.

8. Remove the dough from the pan by lifting it by the paper lining the pan. Cut the loaf in half lengthwise. While holding the 2 halves together, cut the loaf crosswise into ½-inch slices. Each slice should have three stripes. Place the slices 1 inch apart on the prepared baking sheet.

9. Bake for 10 to 12 minutes, or until the edges are light brown. Cool for 2 minutes on the baking sheet, then transfer the cookies to a cooling rack. Cool completely. Store in an airtight container at room temperature for up to 1 week.

STORAGE TIP: The baked cookies may be frozen for up to 3 months in an airtight container. The dough, after it's been layered and cut, may be frozen, keeping the loaf all together, for up to 3 months. Defrost in the refrigerator.

VARIATION: You can make these cookies with other colors and flavors. How about orange, blue raspberry, and pink lemonade? Your combinations are limited only by what colors and extracts are available and your imagination.

TRADITIONS: These cookies are thought to be from Naples, Italy; hence the name Neapolitan. If you've ever had Neapolitan ice cream, you know it's made with similar flavors: chocolate, strawberry, and vanilla.

St. Nicholas Cookies

(SPECULAAS)

Makes 4 dozen cookies

PREP TIME: 25 minutes, plus 2 hours to chill | **COOK TIME:** 10 minutes
Freezer-Friendly, Rolled Cookies

These crispy cinnamon-and-spice cookies, made with a wooden mold that has a design carved into it, are some of my favorites. It's no wonder that several countries claim these cookies as their own. The Dutch know them as speculaas; in Belgium, as *speculoos*; and in Germany, as *spekulatius* cookies. In the United States, most of us know them as biscoff cookies, after the Lotus Biscoff brand out of Europe.

4 cups flour, plus more
for dusting

1 teaspoon baking powder

¼ teaspoon salt

1 tablespoon
ground cinnamon

2 teaspoons
pumpkin pie spice

1 cup (2 sticks)
salted butter, at
room temperature

1½ cups firmly packed
light brown sugar

3 large eggs

1 teaspoon cinnamon
extract

1. In a medium bowl, using a wire whisk, thoroughly combine the flour, baking powder, salt, cinnamon, and pumpkin pie spice. Set aside. In a large bowl, cream the butter and brown sugar together. Add the eggs one at a time, mixing well after each addition. Add the flour mixture ¼ cup at a time until it is completely incorporated.

2. Divide the dough into 4 balls. Wrap each dough ball in plastic wrap and refrigerate for at least 2 hours or up to 24 hours.

3. Preheat the oven to 350°F. Line two baking sheets with parchment paper. Set aside.

4. Lightly flour a work surface. Roll out one ball of dough to ¼ inch thick. Use a knife dusted with flour to cut rectangles or strips, and press them with a speculaas mold. Another option is to cut the dough with cookie cutters dipped in flour.

> RECIPE CONTINUED

5. Place the speculaas on the prepared baking sheets. Two baking sheets may be baked at the same time if they are placed on separate racks. Halfway through the baking process, the baking sheets must be switched from one rack to the other and rotated 180° for even baking.

6. Bake for 10 minutes, or until the cookies are slightly darker and very fragrant.

7. Cool for 2 minutes on the baking sheets, then transfer the cookies to a cooling rack. Cool completely. Repeat with the remaining dough balls. These cookies keep their crunchiness in a container with a loose lid, like a cookie jar or a casserole dish with a glass lid. They keep for up to 1 week at room temperature.

STORAGE TIP: The baked cookies and plastic-wrapped dough both will keep for up to 3 months stored in an airtight container in the freezer. Defrost in the refrigerator.

TECHNIQUE TIP: Have you seen those really intricate rolling pins with designs carved into them? They are perfect for making speculaas. To do this, roll out the dough with a regular rolling pin, then roll the carved pin over the dough. Cut the imprinted dough into squares using a knife or into other shapes using cookie cutters.

Orange-Walnut Biscotti

Makes 2 dozen cookies

PREP TIME: 30 minutes | **COOK TIME:** 40 minutes

Contains Nuts, Freezer-Friendly, Molded Cookies

Biscotti means "twice-baked" in Italian. Don't let the twice-baking portion stop you from trying these delightful cookies. They are so simple to make. I am constantly getting requests for this recipe and always have some on hand for houseguests. They are perfect with afternoon coffee and tea. Lots of people on our Christmas list get these cookies as their gift.

Cooking spray

2½ cups flour

¾ teaspoon
   baking powder

½ teaspoon salt

12 tablespoons
   salted butter, at
   room temperature

1 cup sugar

2 large eggs

1½ teaspoons
   orange extract

Grated zest of 1 orange
   or 2 tangerines

1 cup chopped walnuts,
   lightly toasted

1. Preheat the oven to 350°F. Coat a baking sheet with cooking spray. Set aside.

2. In a medium bowl, using a wire whisk, combine the flour, baking powder, and salt. Set aside. In a large bowl, cream the butter until fluffy. Slowly add the sugar until combined. Add the eggs one at a time, mixing well after each addition. Mix in the orange extract. Gradually add the flour mixture to the butter mixture. Combine completely. Hand-stir in the orange zest and walnuts.

3. Divide the dough in half. With wet hands, shape each half into a 12-inch log. Place them on the prepared baking sheet. Flatten the tops until the logs are 1 inch tall. Bake for 30 minutes, until they are light brown.

4. Place the baking sheet on cooling rack. Cool for about 15 minutes.

> RECIPE CONTINUED

5. Carefully, using a serrated knife, cut the logs into ½- to 1-inch-thick slices. Lay the slices back on the baking sheet. Bake for 5 more minutes, until they are light brown on top. Remove from the oven and flip the cookies. Bake for 5 more minutes, until the other sides are light brown.

6. Cool for 2 minutes on the baking sheet, then transfer the cookies to a cooling rack. Cool completely. Store in an airtight container at room temperature for up to 1 week.

STORAGE TIP: You can freeze the baked cookies, but I prefer to freeze the dough, as the cookies get a bit soft after thawing. After shaping the logs, wrap them in plastic wrap and store in an airtight container or bag for up to 3 months. Defrost in the refrigerator.

TECHNIQUE TIP: Although a serrated knife can be used to slice the baked logs, I've found that an electric knife works even better. I have a designated biscotti baking sheet because the electric knife leaves marks on it.

Linzer Cookies

Makes 24 cookies for 12 sandwiches

PREP TIME: 35 minutes, plus 1 hour to chill | **COOK TIME:** 10 minutes
Rolled Cookies

These shortbread sandwich cookies are named after the Linzer torte, which originated in Linz, Austria, and looks similar to deep-dish fruit pie with a lattice crust. The most common filling is raspberry jam, but you may choose any flavor you like. I've even used mint jelly so I'd have both green- and red-filled cookie windows. Having a set of Linzer cookie cutters is helpful but not necessary (see Technique tip).

2 cups flour, plus ¼ cup for dusting

¼ teaspoon salt

8 tablespoons salted butter, at room temperature

½ cup confectioners' sugar, sifted, plus more for dusting

1 teaspoon vanilla extract

Cooking spray

¼ cup seedless raspberry jam, strawberry jam, or another flavor of jam

1. In a small bowl, using a wire whisk, combine the flour and salt. Set aside. In a large bowl, cream the butter and the confectioners' sugar together. Mix in the vanilla. Gradually mix in the flour mixture until it is well combined.

2. Divide the dough in half. Roll into balls and flatten into oval shapes. Wrap the disks of dough in plastic wrap. Chill in the refrigerator for at least 1 hour and up to 24 hours.

3. When the dough is almost done chilling, put the remaining ¼ cup flour in a small bowl and dust your work surface and rolling pin.

4. Preheat the oven to 350°F. Lightly coat two baking sheets with cooking spray. Set aside.

> RECIPE CONTINUED

5. Remove 1 dough disk, leaving the other one in the refrigerator. Roll it out to ¼-inch thickness. Using 2-inch Linzer cookie cutters, cut out 12 cookies. Repeat with the other disk of dough. Half the cookies should have a hole in the center; these are the top halves. The other half should remain whole cookies; these are the bottom halves. Place the cookies 1 inch apart on the prepared cookie sheets. Two baking sheets may be baked at the same time if they are placed on separate racks. Halfway through the baking process, the sheets must be switched from one rack to the other and rotated 180° for even baking.

6. Bake for 7 to 9 minutes or until the edges are brown. Cool for 2 minutes on the baking sheet, then transfer the cookies to a cooling rack. Cool completely.

7. Lay out a piece of wax paper on a work surface. Place the top cookie halves on the wax paper and sift confectioners' sugar over them.

8. On each bottom cookie half, spread 1 teaspoon of jam. Top them with the top halves. Store in an airtight container at room temperature; the cookies will begin to soften after a couple of days.

TECHNIQUE TIP: You don't have to buy Linzer cookie cutters to make these. All you need are two cookie cutters, one half the size of the other, to punch the centers out. Heart cookie cutters are the easiest to find in various sizes.

Holiday Shortbread Biscuits

Makes 4 dozen biscuits

PREP TIME: 25 minutes | **COOK TIME:** 30 minutes

Bar Cookies, Freezer-Friendly

The English cherish the tradition of "biscuits" (what we call cookies) and tea. These biscuits are more than just shortbread. They are made extra special by dipping them in white or dark chocolate and topping with nonpareils. Shortbread in pretty tins is widely available for purchase at Christmastime. What makes this shortbread extra special is that it is homemade.

2½ cups flour

½ cup sugar

1 cup (2 sticks) cold salted butter

1 cup white or dark chocolate chips

1 tablespoon vegetable shortening or coconut oil

Nonpareils, such as sprinkles or any other type

1. Preheat the oven to 350°F.

2. In a large bowl, using a wire whisk, combine the flour and sugar. Cut the butter into small cubes and add them to the flour mixture. Use a pastry blender, two knives, or your hands to blend the butter into the mixture. The mixture should look like little peas and there shouldn't be patches of loose flour.

3. Press the mixture into an ungreased 9-by-13-inch baking pan. Pat it down evenly.

4. Bake for 25 to 30 minutes or until brown around the edges and on top. Cool for 30 minutes, then cut the shortbread into squares and cut the squares diagonally. Cool for another 30 minutes.

5. Once the shortbread is completely cool, put the chocolate chips and shortening in a microwave-safe bowl. Microwave for 30 seconds. Stir. If the chips aren't completely melted, heat for another 20 seconds. Stir and repeat another 10 seconds if necessary.

6. Lay a piece of parchment paper on the kitchen counter. Place an empty cereal bowl on the paper. Dip a corner of a biscuit into the chocolate. Holding the freshly dipped shortbread over the empty bowl, sprinkle it with nonpareils, allowing any extra to fall in the bowl.

7. Store in an airtight container for up to 1 week. They may get softer under the chocolate portion.

STORAGE TIP: The baked, undipped shortbread can be frozen for up to 3 months in an airtight container.

TECHNIQUE TIP: To use two knives to cut the butter in, hold one in each hand with their blades facing each other. Push the knives together as if they were a pair of scissors, cutting through the butter and flour mixture. Continue cutting until the mixture has the consistency of little peas. Or you can use a food processor. Put the flour and sugar in the processor bowl. Add the butter and pulse until you have the proper consistency. Use a silicone spatula to transfer it to your baking sheet. Follow the recipe from step 3.

VARIATION: There will come a day when you want to bake cookies and think you don't have the ingredients to make them. Fear not—all you need to make shortbread is flour, sugar, and butter. Simply combine those ingredients as directed and follow the baking instructions. You'll have buttery, rich cookies in no time.

Polish-Style Christmas Cookies

(KOLACZKI)

Makes 4 dozen cookies

PREP TIME: 40 minutes, plus 2 hours to chill | **COOK TIME:** 15 minutes
Freezer-Friendly, Rolled Cookies

Croatia and the Czech Republic also lay claim to this jam-filled cookie. There are multiple ways of making them; this is my favorite. The fillings may vary, as well, ranging from different-flavored jams, like strawberry and apricot, to nuts and chocolate (see Variation tip for more options). I chose raspberry jam for the flavor and the color.

- **1½ cups (3 sticks) salted butter, at room temperature**
- **1 (8-ounce) package cream cheese, at room temperature**
- **3 cups flour, divided**
- **½ teaspoon salt**
- **½ cup confectioners' sugar**
- **1 cup seedless raspberry jam**

TRADITIONS: Christmas-time is when you're likely to find trays of kolaczki in the homes of Polish Americans, a lovely way to remember those family members who are no longer with us.

STORAGE TIP: Freeze the plastic-wrapped dough for up to 3 months in an airtight container. Defrost in the refrigerator.

1. In a large bowl, cream the butter and cream cheese together until light and fluffy. Add 1 cup of flour and sprinkle the salt all over. Mix until combined. Add the remaining 2 cups of flour 1 cup at a time, making sure all of the flour is completely combined.

2. Form the dough into a ball. Flatten it slightly and wrap it completely in plastic wrap. Refrigerate the dough for at least 2 hours or up to 24 hours. If storing the dough in the refrigerator overnight, place the wrapped dough in a resealable bag, as well.

3. Preheat the oven to 350°F. Line a baking sheet with parchment paper. Set aside. Measure the confectioners' sugar into a mesh strainer placed over a bowl.

4. Prepare a work surface to roll out the dough: Sift confectioners' sugar lightly over the work surface. Sift a little more onto a rolling pin. Place a small bowl of water nearby.

5. Divide the dough in half and place one half on the work surface. Put the remaining dough back

into the refrigerator. Sift confectioners' sugar over the top of the dough. Turn it over and sift confectioners' sugar over the other side. Roll out the dough until it's ¼ inch thick. Using a knife, cut as many 2-inch squares as possible. Place the squares on the prepared baking sheets.

6. Place 1 teaspoon of the raspberry jam in the center of each square. Use the spoon to spread the jam diagonally from one corner to the opposite corner, going almost to the edges.

7. Wet one of your fingers in the water bowl and pull one uncovered corner toward the other uncovered corner, folding them over each other to seal. Use more water if necessary to keep the corners together.

8. Bake for 12 to 15 minutes, or until the edges are light brown and the centers are slightly bubbly. Remove from the oven and sift confectioners' sugar over all of the cookies. Cool for 2 minutes on the baking sheet, then transfer the cookies to a cooling rack. Cool completely. Repeat with the other half of the dough. Store in an airtight container at room temperature for up to 1 week.

VARIATION: Besides other jam flavors, you can use canned fillings, like plum, raspberry, and poppy seed (see Resources, page 146). The most traditional filling is apricot. To make it, place 1 cup dried apricots in a large saucepan with 1 cup water. Add 2 tablespoons sugar and 3 tablespoons lemon juice. Bring to a boil and simmer for 15 minutes. Most of the liquid should be absorbed. Remove from the heat and mash the fruit by hand or in a food processor. Allow the filling to cool completely before using.

Snowballs

Makes 3 dozen cookies

PREP TIME: 30 minutes, plus 2 hours to chill | **COOK TIME:** 20 minutes

Contains Nuts, Freezer-Friendly, Molded Cookies

Snowballs are also called Russian Tea Cakes, Danish Wedding Cookies, Mexican Wedding Cookies, and Pecan Cookies. They are a butter-and-pecan-flavored cookie rolled in confectioners' sugar twice, both before and after baking.

2 cups flour

½ teaspoon salt

1 cup finely chopped lightly toasted pecans

1 cup (2 sticks) salted butter, at room temperature

1½ cups confectioners' sugar, divided

1 teaspoon vanilla extract

1 teaspoon almond extract

INGREDIENT TIP: It is easier to chop nuts after they've been toasted. In this recipe especially, it's very important to make sure the pecans are finely chopped. If the pieces are too big, it may affect the size of the cookies.

STORAGE TIP: Snowballs can be frozen for up to 3 months in an airtight container.

1. In a small bowl, using a wire whisk, combine the flour and salt and stir in the pecans. Set aside. In a large bowl, cream the butter and ½ cup of confectioners' sugar together. Mix in the extracts. Slowly add the flour mixture, ½ cup at a time, until completely combined.

2. Wrap the ball of dough in plastic wrap. Refrigerate the dough for at least 2 hours.

3. Preheat the oven to 325°F. Line two baking sheets with parchment paper. Set aside.

4. Put the remaining 1 cup of confectioners' sugar in a low-sided bowl. Form the dough into 2-inch balls. Roll each ball in the confectioners' sugar. Place the cookies on the prepared baking sheets. Two baking sheets may be baked at the same time if they are placed on separate racks. Halfway through the baking process, the baking sheets must be switched from one rack to the other and rotated 180° for even baking.

5. Bake for 15 to 20 minutes, or until light brown. Cool for 2 minutes on the baking sheets, then transfer the cookies to cooling racks. Once cool enough to handle, roll them in the confectioners' sugar one more time. Store in an airtight container at room temperature for up to 1 week.

Sprinkle Cookies

Makes 20 cookies

PREP TIME: 1 hour 30 minutes | **COOK TIME:** 15 minutes

Freezer-Friendly, Molded Cookies

Over the Christmas holidays, we like to go to New England to visit my husband's family. Almost everyone we visit has a plate or two of these traditional Italian cookies to share. At our wedding, my soon-to-be mother-in-law and sister-in-law brought a basket of them along with other Italian cookies. There wasn't a cookie left after the festivities. These aren't overly sweet; most of the sweetness comes from the vanilla glaze and sprinkles.

FOR THE COOKIES

3 cups flour

1 tablespoon
   baking powder

½ teaspoon salt

8 tablespoons
   salted butter, at
   room temperature

½ cup granulated sugar

3 large eggs

1½ teaspoons
   vanilla extract

¼ teaspoon almond or
   anise extract

FOR THE ICING

2 cups confectioners'
   sugar, sifted

2 to 3 tablespoons cream,
   milk, or water

½ teaspoon vanilla extract

¼ teaspoon almond or
   anise extract

3 tablespoons
   multicolored sprinkles

TO MAKE THE COOKIES

1. In a small bowl, using a wire whisk, combine the flour, baking powder, and salt. Set aside. In a large bowl, cream the butter and granulated sugar together. Add the eggs one at a time, mixing well after each addition. Add the vanilla extract and almond extract. Mix completely. Add the flour mixture ½ cup at a time to the butter mixture, mixing completely after each addition.

2. Line a baking sheet with parchment paper.

3. Measure out 2 tablespoons of dough at a time. Using wet hands, roll the dough into balls. Place the balls on the prepared baking sheet. Place the baking sheet in the refrigerator for 1 hour.

4. Preheat the oven to 350°F.

5. Bake for 10 to 12 minutes, or until the cookies are lightly browned. Cool for 5 minutes on the baking sheet, then transfer the cookies to a cooling rack positioned over a newspaper- or wax paper–covered surface. Cool completely.

TO MAKE THE ICING

6. In a medium bowl, whisk together the confectioners' sugar, 2 tablespoons of cream, the vanilla extract, and almond extract. If the icing seems too thick, add up to 1 more tablespoon of cream. Spoon half of the icing over half of the cookies and decorate them with sprinkles. Drizzling the remaining icing over the rest of the cookies and top with the rest of the sprinkles. Before serving, allow the icing to set. This will take about an hour. Store in an airtight container at room temperature for up to 1 week.

   INGREDIENT TIP: Don't be afraid to try using anise extract instead of almond. The licorice flavor will not be overwhelming.

   STORAGE TIP: The baked cookies or plastic-wrapped dough will keep in an airtight container in the freezer for up to 3 months. Freeze the cookies before frosting them. Frost them once they are at room temperature. Defrost the dough in the refrigerator.

Chocolate-Dipped Almond Cookies

(AMYGDALOTA)

Makes 1 dozen cookies

PREP TIME: 25 minutes | **COOK TIME:** 15 minutes

Contains Nuts, Molded Cookies

My Greek mother-in-law has taught me a lot about her traditional pastries. She's taken me to many Greek festivals where most of the money raised for the local church is from selling wonderfully delicious traditional cookies, like these crescent-shaped almond cookies. In addition to Christmastime, amygda-lota ("ah-MIG-dah-low-ta") are often served at baptisms and weddings. To the Greeks, almonds symbolize new beginnings and prosperity. Personally, I find the smell of them baking intoxicating. Of course, their light, chewy texture isn't bad, either!

1 cup sliced almonds, coarsely crushed (see Technique tip)

2 large egg whites, separated

½ cup almond flour

⅓ cup sugar

¼ teaspoon salt

1 (7- to 8-ounce) package almond paste

1 teaspoon almond extract

½ cup dark chocolate chips

1 teaspoon vegetable shortening or coconut oil

Nonpareils, such as multicolored sprinkles (optional)

1. Preheat the oven to 375°F. Line a baking sheet with parchment paper. Set aside.

2. Place the almonds in a low-sided bowl at least 5 inches in diameter and set aside. In another low-sided bowl, place 1 egg white. Using a fork, beat it just a little and set aside.

3. In a small bowl, using a wire whisk, combine the almond flour, sugar, and salt. Set aside. In a large, deep bowl, pinch off 1-inch pieces of almond paste until the entire package is used. Add the remaining egg white and the almond extract and beat together with an electric mixer. Add the flour mixture and mix until well incorporated. You shouldn't see any loose flour. This is not a smooth dough. It will look like a bowl of soft, large, beige chunks.

4. Grab a couple of the dough chunks and press them together to form a 1½-inch ball. With your fingers, shape it into a 3½- to 4-inch log. Roll the log in the egg white, then place the log in the bowl of almonds. Sprinkle almonds all over the log until it's well covered. Form the log into a crescent shape and place it on the prepared baking sheet. Repeat until the sheet is filled, placing the cookies 1 inch apart.

5. Bake the cookies for 12 to 14 minutes, or until golden brown. Cool on the baking sheet for 2 minutes, then transfer the cookies to a cooling rack. Cool completely.

6. In a microwave-safe bowl, microwave the chocolate and shortening for 30 seconds. Stir. If not melted, microwave for another 20 seconds and stir. Add another 10 seconds if needed.

7. Place a large piece of parchment or wax paper on the kitchen counter. Dip an end of each cookie into the melted chocolate. If desired, the chocolate ends could be dipped in colored sprinkles, then allowed to dry on the paper. Otherwise, place the cookies on the paper after dipping the ends in the chocolate. Once fully dry, store in an airtight container at room temperature for up to 1 week.

TECHNIQUE TIP: To crush the almonds, pour them into a quart-size resealable bag. Seal the bag and use the heels of your hands to crush the almonds. They will end up in thirds or quarters.

VARIATION: All-purpose flour can be used instead of almond flour. Or a combination of ¼ cup all-purpose flour and ¼ cup whole-wheat flour is another acceptable substitution for the almond flour.

Chocolate-Dipped Macaroons

Makes 12 to 14 macaroons

PREP TIME: 15 minutes | **COOK TIME:** 20 minutes

Contains Nuts, Freezer-Friendly, Molded Cookies

Macaroons are one of my daughter's favorite cookies. She is a purist. She prefers them plain—no sprinkles, no nuts, no chocolate. Macaroons are all about the look, smell, and taste. Pick one up and instantly you can smell the tropics. Bite into it and you'll find it's a bit crunchy on the outside and soft and chewy on the inside. These make a nice changeup to the typical Christmas cookie selections.

5⅓ cups sweetened shredded coconut

1 (14-ounce) can sweetened condensed milk

2 teaspoons vanilla extract

2 large egg whites, room temperature

¼ teaspoon sea salt

1 (6-ounce) bag semisweet chocolate chips

1 tablespoon vegetable or refined coconut oil

1 cup crushed almonds (optional)

Sprinkles (optional)

1. Preheat the oven to 350°F. Line a baking sheet with parchment paper. Set aside.

2. In a large bowl, mix together the coconut, condensed milk, and vanilla. In a small bowl, using an electric mixer, beat the egg whites and salt until the whites form stiff peaks. Using a silicone spatula, gently fold the egg whites into the coconut mixture.

3. Scoop out the cookie dough by the tablespoon into your hands and roll into balls. Place the balls on the prepared baking sheet 1 inch apart.

4. Bake for 20 minutes, or until the edges are brown. Cool for 5 minutes on the baking sheet, then transfer the cookies to a cooling rack.

5. Meanwhile, prepare a parchment paper–covered surface for the chocolate on the cookies to set. Pour almonds and/or sprinkles (if using) into a low-sided bowl or bowls to allow for optional dipping.

> RECIPE CONTINUED

6. Once the cookies are cool, add the chocolate chips and oil to a microwave-safe bowl and microwave for 30 seconds. Stir. If there are still whole chips, continue to microwave for 10- to 20-second periods, stirring in between, until all of the chips are melted.

7. Dip the macaroons in the melted chocolate so they are partially covered. Dip the chocolate part in the almonds and/or sprinkles (if using). Place the macaroons on the parchment paper. When set, store in an airtight container at room temperature for up to 1 week.

INGREDIENT TIP: When melting the chocolate chips, be sure not to use olive oil, as it will impart a distinct flavor that won't go well with your cookies. Both vegetable oil and refined coconut oil are flavorless. It takes only 10 to 20 seconds in the microwave to liquify coconut oil.

STORAGE TIP: The baked cookies will keep in an airtight container in the freezer for up to 3 months.

TROUBLESHOOTING TIP: Be very careful when using the microwave to melt chocolate. Heat it too long and it will "seize" and get hard. There is no way to fix it once it happens. This is the reason I start with 30 seconds, then shorten the timing each time I need to put it back until it's melted. If there are just a few chips left in the chocolate, stir it and wait a couple of minutes before heating again.

Chinese-Style Almond Cookies

Makes 2 dozen cookies

PREP TIME: 25 minutes | **COOK TIME:** 15 minutes

Contains Nuts, Freezer-Friendly, Molded Cookies

Traditionally, after a long day of Christmas shopping, my mother, dad, and I would eat dinner at the local Chinese restaurant. We'd feast on everything from hot tea to dessert. Besides the obligatory fortune cookie and orange slice, we also got yummy almond cookies for dessert. They are such a simple, not-overly-sweet cookie, with just a hint of almond. Actually, there are no nuts in these cookies, just the one found on top. The almond flavor comes from extract.

Cooking spray

1 egg white

1 tablespoon water

3¼ cups flour, divided

1 teaspoon baking powder

½ teaspoon salt

1 cup (2 sticks) salted butter, at room temperature

1 cup sugar

1 large egg

1½ teaspoons almond extract

24 blanched almonds

1. Preheat the oven to 325°F. Lightly coat two baking sheets with cooking spray. Set aside.

2. In a low-sided bowl, beat the egg white with the water. In a separate low-sided bowl, place ¼ cup of flour. Set the bowls aside.

3. In a medium bowl, using a wire whisk, combine the remaining 3 cups of flour, the baking powder, and salt. Set aside. In a large bowl, cream the butter and sugar together. Add the egg and almond extract. Combine completely. Slowly mix in the flour mixture ½ cup at a time until completely combined.

4. Form the cookie dough into 2-inch balls and place them 2 inches apart on the prepared baking sheets. Use a holiday cookie press or the bottom of a glass dipped in flour to press the tops of the dough balls. Paint each cookie with the egg white mixture and top with 1 blanched almond. Two baking sheets may be baked at the same time if they are placed on separate racks.

> RECIPE CONTINUED

Halfway through the baking process, the sheets must be switched from one rack to the other and rotated 180° for even baking.

5. Bake for 12 to 14 minutes, until the edges are slightly browned. Cool 2 minutes on the baking sheets, then transfer the cookies to a cooling rack. Cool completely. The cookies keep for up to 1 week. Store them in a loose-fitting cookie jar for a crispy cookie. If preferred, these cookies will become softer in an airtight container.

STORAGE TIP: The plastic-wrapped dough and baked cookies freeze beautifully in an airtight container for up to 3 months. Defrost in the refrigerator.

TECHNIQUE TIP: You can use just about anything with a flat bottom to flatten the dough. Juice glasses are perfect. I use a cookie press with a design sunk into it. If you use a cookie press, be sure to choose one that has a design that the almond will look good pressed into.

Classic Chocolate Chip Cookies

Makes 5 dozen cookies

PREP TIME: 30 minutes | **COOK TIME:** 15 minutes

Bar Cookies, Drop Cookies, Freezer-Friendly

Even though these aren't traditional Christmas cookies, you will find plenty of them being made, and consumed, during this time of year. This is the one cookie recipe that should be in everyone's baking repertoire. Everything will be forgiven if you can make excellent chocolate chip cookies like these. Plan it right, and you should be able to bake these cookies anytime. I try to keep the dough in my freezer at all times for that reason, frozen into individual balls, so I only have to pull out the number of cookies I want to bake.

2¼ cups flour

1 teaspoon salt

1 teaspoon baking soda

1 cup (2 sticks) salted butter, at room temperature

1 cup firmly packed light brown sugar

½ cup granulated sugar

2 large eggs

1 teaspoon vanilla extract

2 cups semisweet chocolate chips

1 cup coarsely chopped lightly toasted pecans (optional)

1. Preheat the oven to 375°F. Line two baking sheets with parchment paper. Set aside.

2. In a medium bowl, using a wire whisk, combine the flour, salt, and baking soda. Set aside. In a large bowl, cream the butter, brown sugar, and granulated sugar together until light and fluffy. Beat in the eggs one at a time. Add the vanilla and make sure the dough is well mixed. Hand-stir in the chocolate chips and pecans (if using).

3. Measure out the dough 1 rounded tablespoon at a time and place on the prepared baking sheets. Two baking sheets may be baked at the same time if they are placed on separate racks. Halfway through the baking process, the baking sheets must be switched from one rack to the other and rotated 180° for even baking.

> RECIPE CONTINUED

4. Bake for 9 to 11 minutes, or until the cookies are golden brown and you can smell them. Cool for 2 minutes on the baking sheets, then transfer the cookies to cooling racks. Cool completely. These store best in a cookie jar with a loose lid for up to 1 week.

STORAGE TIP: The baked cookies keep for up to 3 months in the freezer in an airtight container. To freeze the dough, roll it into 1- or 2-tablespoon-size balls, freeze overnight on a baking sheet, then transfer to a freezer bag for storage. They can be baked frozen; just add a few more minutes to the baking time.

TECHNIQUE TIP: Want these cookies in a hurry without having to bake them in batches? Press the dough into an even layer in lightly greased jelly roll pan. Bake at 350°F for 20 to 25 minutes. Once cool, cut the cookies into squares.

VARIATION: To add a Christmas spin to these cookies, substitute 1 cup Christmas candy-coated chocolates for either the nuts or half of the chocolate chips.

Peanut Butter Blossoms

Makes 4 dozen cookies

PREP TIME: 25 minutes | **COOK TIME:** 10 minutes
Contains Nuts, Freezer-Friendly, Molded Cookies

These cookies are so simple to make—all you need to do is to press a chocolate kiss down into each of the peanut butter balls freshly removed from the oven. Once they're cool, they are ready to eat. I don't believe I've ever been to a Christmas cookie swap or holiday party where someone didn't bring these cookies. It makes sense as there aren't many who can pass up that chocolate-and-peanut-butter flavor combination, including myself.

1½ cups flour

1 teaspoon baking soda

½ teaspoon salt

8 tablespoons salted butter

¾ cup peanut butter

⅔ cup granulated sugar, divided

⅓ cup firmly packed light brown sugar

1 large egg

2 tablespoons milk

1 teaspoon vanilla extract

48 Hershey's Kisses milk chocolates, unwrapped

1. Preheat the oven to 375°F. Line two baking sheets with parchment paper. Set aside. In a medium bowl, using a wire whisk, combine the flour, baking soda, and salt. Set aside. In a large bowl, cream the butter, peanut butter, ⅓ cup of granulated sugar, and the brown sugar together. Add the egg and mix in. Stir in the milk and vanilla. Add the flour mixture, ½ cup at a time, mixing after each addition until well combined.

2. Shape the dough into 1-inch balls. Roll the balls in the remaining ⅓ cup granulated sugar and place on the prepared baking sheets. Two baking sheets may be baked at the same time if they are placed on separate racks. Halfway through the baking process, the baking sheets must be switched from one rack to the other and rotated 180° for even baking.

3. Bake for 8 to 10 minutes, or until lightly brown. As soon as they are out of the oven, press a Kiss into the center of each cookie. The edges of the cookies may crack. Transfer the cookies to a cooling rack for cooling. Store in an airtight container at room temperature for up to 1 week.

STORAGE TIP: The dough can be frozen in an airtight container for up to 3 months. Defrost in the refrigerator. Freezing the baked cookies is not recommended as the Kisses will turn ashy white—it doesn't hurt the flavor but it's not pretty to look at.

VARIATION: Hershey's Kisses are still a favorite, but there are other candies that will work with these cookies, like chocolate–peanut butter candies; chocolate, peanut, and nougat candies; chocolate-nougat candy bars—even the leftovers from a box of chocolates could work. Just remember that the different flavors should complement the peanut butter cookie.

Chocolate Crinkles

Makes 3 dozen cookies

PREP TIME: 30 minutes, plus 3 hours to chill | **COOK TIME:** 15 minutes

Freezer-Friendly, Molded Cookies

Chocolate crinkles stand out on every Christmas cookie board or at a cookie swap. Making these is very similar to making brownies. If the base recipe hasn't got enough chocolate for you, add the optional chocolate chips.

2 cups flour

¾ cup granulated sugar

2 teaspoons
baking powder

½ teaspoon salt

½ cup vegetable oil

4 ounces unsweetened
chocolate, melted
and cooled

4 large eggs,
slightly beaten

2 teaspoons
vanilla extract

1 cup mini chocolate
chips (optional)

1 cup confectioners' sugar

STORAGE TIP: The baked cookies will keep for up to 3 months frozen in an airtight container.

TECHNIQUE TIP: It's very important to not overbake these. The outsides are supposed to be slightly hard and the center should still be a little fudgy.

1. In a large bowl, using a wire whisk, combine the flour, granulated sugar, baking powder, and salt. Stir in the vegetable oil, unsweetened chocolate, eggs, and vanilla. Carefully stir in the chocolate chips (if using). Don't overmix the ingredients.

2. Refrigerate at least 3 hours or up to 24 hours.

3. Preheat the oven to 350°F. Line two baking sheets with parchment paper. Set aside.

4. Sift the confectioners' sugar into low-sided bowl. Roll 1 tablespoon of dough into a ball. Drop the ball into the sugar. Roll it around until it is completely covered. Place the ball on a prepared baking sheet. Repeat until both baking sheets are full. Refrigerate any remaining dough until it's ready to be baked. Two baking sheets may be baked at the same time if they are placed on separate racks. Halfway through the baking, the sheets must be switched from one rack to the other and rotated 180° for even baking.

5. Bake for 10 to 12 minutes, or until no indentation remains when touched. Cool for 2 minutes on the baking sheets, then transfer them to a cooling rack. Cool completely. Repeat with the remaining dough. Store in an airtight container at room temperature for up to 1 week.

CHAPTER THREE

Classics with a Twist

Christmastime isn't just for the gingerbread and spritz cookies of the world. Any of your favorite cookies can be enjoyed at this time of year—you just need to update them with the holiday spirit! When I think of Christmas, I think of the color red and cranberries. How about some Oatmeal Cranberry Cookies? As pretty as sugar cookies are, how about ones that look like stained-glass windows? Almost everyone loves peanut butter cookies, so why not make them with extra nuts and holiday-colored candy? Most snickerdoodles have only cinnamon on the inside, but these holiday Ultimate Snickerdoodles feature three kinds of cinnamon, inside and out! Check out this chapter for amped-up holiday versions of the classics.

Oatmeal-Cranberry Cookies

Makes 4 dozen cookies

PREP TIME: 30 minutes | **COOK TIME:** 10 minutes

Bar Cookies, Drop Cookies, Freezer-Friendly

It's hard to find a more well-loved cookie than an oatmeal cookie. Cranberries lend a sweet-tart flavor to an already delicately sweet oatmeal cookie, making it the perfect Christmas treat. Did you know you can make these cookies all year long? If fresh cranberries are out of season, look for them in the frozen fruit section.

1½ cups flour

1 teaspoon baking soda

1 teaspoon ground cinnamon

¾ teaspoon salt

1¼ cups (2½ sticks) salted butter, at room temperature

¾ cup firmly packed light brown sugar

¾ cup granulated sugar

1 large egg

1 teaspoon vanilla extract

3 cups old-fashioned rolled oats

1 cup fresh cranberries

1. Preheat the oven to 375°F. Line two baking sheets with parchment paper.

2. In a medium bowl, using a wire whisk, combine the flour, baking soda, cinnamon, and salt. Set aside. In a large bowl, cream the butter, brown sugar, and granulated sugar together until light and fluffy. Mix in the egg and the vanilla. Hand-stir in the oats until combined. Finally, hand-stir in the cranberries.

3. Measure out 1 heaping tablespoon of cookie dough and place on a prepared baking sheet. Fill both of the baking sheets, allowing for 2 inches in between cookies. Place the remaining cookie dough in the refrigerator. Two baking sheets may be baked at the same time if they are placed on separate racks. Halfway through the baking process, the baking sheets must be switched from one rack to the other and rotated 180° for even baking.

> RECIPE CONTINUED

4. Bake for 8 to 10 minutes, or until the edges are light brown. Cool for 2 minutes on the baking sheet, then transfer the cookies to a cooling rack. Cool completely. Repeat with the remaining cookie dough. Store the cookies in a cookie jar with a loose lid. These will last up to 1 week in the cookie jar.

INGREDIENT TIP: Frozen cranberries can be used. If necessary, with the bag still sealed, gently separate the frozen cranberries. Hand-stir the frozen cranberries into the batter. Add 2 to 3 minutes to the baking time. You can also substitute dried cranberries; the bake time is the same.

STORAGE TIP: You can freeze either the baked cookies or the dough for up to 3 months. Shape the dough into balls, freeze on baking sheets overnight, then transfer to airtight containers. You can bake them straight from the freezer; increase the bake time to 12 to 14 minutes.

VARIATION: You can also bake these as bar cookies. Press the dough into an even layer in a buttered 9-by-13-inch baking sheet. Bake at 350°F for 25 to 30 minutes, or until the edges are brown and the center looks cooked. Cool in the pan completely on a cooling rack before cutting into 24 bars.

Ultimate Snickerdoodles

Makes 4 dozen cookies

PREP TIME: 20 minutes | **COOK TIME:** 10 minutes

Bar Cookies, Drop Cookies, Freezer-Friendly

The smell of cinnamon is everywhere during Christmastime. The only cinnamon found in regular snickerdoodles is on the outside of the cookie, which is typically rolled in a cinnamon-sugar mixture. There are three types of cinnamon in these Ultimate Snickerdoodles: ground cinnamon, cinnamon extract, and cinnamon chips. As far as Christmas cookies go, you can never have too much cinnamon—this warming spice is the perfect antidote to that crisp chill in the winter months.

2¾ cups flour

4 teaspoons ground cinnamon, divided

2 teaspoons cream of tartar

1 teaspoon baking soda

¾ teaspoon salt

1 cup (2 sticks) salted butter, at room temperature

1 cup firmly packed light brown sugar

¾ cup granulated sugar, divided

2 large eggs

1 teaspoon cinnamon extract

1 (10-ounce) package cinnamon chips

1. Preheat the oven to 400°F. Line two baking sheets with parchment paper.

2. In a medium bowl, using a wire whisk, combine the flour, 2 teaspoons of cinnamon, the cream of tartar, baking soda, and salt. Set aside. In a large bowl, cream the butter, brown sugar, and ½ cup of granulated sugar together until light and fluffy. Add the eggs, one at a time, mixing well after each addition. Add the flour mixture ½ cup at a time, mixing after each addition. Add the cinnamon extract and combine completely. Hand-stir in the cinnamon chips.

3. In a low-sided bowl, whisk together the remaining 2 teaspoons of cinnamon and the remaining ¼ cup of granulated sugar.

4. To form the cookies, take 1 tablespoon of the dough and roll into a 1-inch ball. Roll the balls in the cinnamon-sugar mixture and place them on the prepared baking sheets, with 2 inches between them. Two baking sheets may be baked

> RECIPE CONTINUED

at the same time if they are placed on two separate racks. Halfway through the baking process, the baking sheets must be switched from one rack to the other and rotated 180° for even baking.

5. Bake for 6 minutes, or until the edges are light brown. Cool for 2 minutes on the baking sheet, then transfer the cookies to a cooling rack. Cool completely. These will keep for up to 1 week at room temperature. If soft cookies are preferred, store them in an airtight container. If a slightly crisper cookie is preferred, store in a cookie jar with a loose lid.

INGREDIENT TIP: Cinnamon extract is more easily found during the baking season (from Halloween to just after New Year's). When I find it, I may buy a few bottles. If you can't find it, you may use vanilla instead.

STORAGE TIP: The baked cookies or the dough can be frozen for up to 3 months. Shape the dough into balls, freeze on baking sheets overnight, and transfer to airtight containers. Defrost just enough so the surface gets sticky before rolling in the cinnamon sugar. They may take a little longer to bake if still partially frozen.

VARIATION: You can also bake these as bar cookies. Press the dough into an even layer in a buttered 9-by-13-inch baking sheet. Sprinkle the top of the dough evenly with the cinnamon-sugar mixture. Bake at 350°F for 25 to 30 minutes, or until the edges are brown and the center looks cooked.

Crunchy Peanut Butter Cookies

Makes 3 dozen cookies

PREP TIME: 35 minutes | **COOK TIME:** 15 minutes

Contains Nuts, Freezer-Friendly, Molded Cookies

Living in the southern United States, I am no stranger to peanuts. I remember my mother riding in the passenger seat with a towel on her lap during car trips. The towel was there to catch the liquid from the boiled peanuts that we had just bought from a local farm stand. That also brings back memories of coming home from school to freshly baked peanut butter cookies or homemade peanut butter fudge. Peanuts and peanut butter have always been a big part of my life, which is why I love these cookies. The red and green peanut-filled, candy-coated chocolate pieces give these cookies an infusion of Christmas spirit.

¼ cup granulated sugar

1¼ cups flour

1 teaspoon baking soda

½ teaspoon salt

8 tablespooons salted butter, at room temperature

⅔ cup crunchy peanut butter

1 cup firmly packed light brown sugar

2 large eggs

1 teaspoon vanilla extract

2 (10-ounce) bags candy-coated, Christmas-colored, chocolate-covered peanuts, 1 bag coarsely chopped, 1 bag pieces left whole

1. Preheat the oven to 350°F. Line a baking sheet with parchment paper. Set aside. Place the granulated sugar in a low-sided bowl and set aside.

2. In a medium bowl, using a wire whisk, combine the flour, baking soda, and salt. Set aside. In a large bowl, cream the butter, peanut butter, and brown sugar together until light and fluffy. Add the eggs one at a time, mixing well after each addition. Add the vanilla and mix until completely combined. Hand-stir in the chocolate-covered peanuts.

3. Measure out a heaping tablespoon of dough at a time and form each into a ball. Roll the balls in the bowl of granulated sugar and place on the prepared baking sheets at least 2 inches apart. Press the dough down with the bottom of a small glass. Press a couple of whole candy pieces into the top of the cookies.

> RECIPE CONTINUED

4. Bake for 10 to 12 minutes, or until light brown around the edges. Cool for 2 minutes on the baking sheet, then transfer to a cooling rack. Cool completely. For a crispy cookie, store them at room temperature for up to 1 week in a cookie jar with a loose lid. For a softer cookie, store them at room temperature for up to 1 week in an airtight container.

STORAGE TIP: The baked cookies or the dough can be frozen for up to 3 months. Shape the dough into balls, freeze on baking sheets overnight, then transfer to airtight containers. The cookie dough can be baked straight from the freezer; they may need a couple of extra minutes.

TECHNIQUE TIP: A food processor makes chopping the peanuts easy, but if you don't feel like pulling it out or don't have one, put the peanuts in a zip-top plastic bag and seal, then hit with the flat side of a meat hammer until all the candies are broken.

TROUBLESHOOTING TIP: As there is not much flour in this recipe, the dough can be very soft. If you're making these in a warm kitchen, chill the dough for 30 minutes before measuring out the cookies.

Cranberry-Orange Chocolate Linzer Cookies

Makes 24 cookies for 12 sandwiches

PREP TIME: 45 minutes, plus 1 hour to chill | **COOK TIME:** 10 minutes

Rolled Cookies

My husband is a huge orange-chocolate fan and my daughter is a huge cranberry-orange relish fan. I created these cookies by putting their favorites together. From Thanksgiving through New Year's, we always have homemade cranberry-orange relish in the refrigerator. If you don't have time to make your own (see Variation tip), this recipe uses a simplified version made with store-bought marmalade and cranberry sauce. Either way, these are fabulous.

1½ cups flour, plus ¼ cup for dusting

¼ cup unsweetened cocoa powder

8 tablespoons salted butter, at room temperature

½ cup plus 2 tablespoons confectioners' sugar, sifted, plus more for dusting

1¼ teaspoons vanilla extract

¼ cup prepared orange marmalade

2 tablespoons whole-berry cranberry sauce, drained if necessary

Cooking spray

1. In a small bowl, using a wire whisk, combine 1½ cups of flour, the cocoa, and salt. Set aside. In a large bowl, cream the butter and confectioners' sugar together. Mix in the vanilla. Gradually mix in the flour mixture until it is well combined.

2. Divide the dough in half. Roll into large balls and flatten into oval shapes. Wrap the two pieces of dough in plastic wrap. Refrigerate the dough for at least 1 hour or up to 24 hours.

3. While the dough chills, in a small bowl, combine the orange marmalade and whole-berry cranberry sauce, making sure to crush the whole berries. Set aside.

4. Preheat the oven to 350°F. Lightly coat two baking sheets with cooking spray. Set aside.

> RECIPE CONTINUED

5. Put the remaining ¼ cup of flour in a low-sided bowl. Flour your work surface and your rolling pin. Remove 1 dough disk from the refrigerator. Roll it out to ¼-inch thickness, and using 2-inch Linzer cookie cutters, cut out 12 cookies. Repeat with the other disk of dough. Half of the cookies should have a hole in the center; these are the top halves. The other half should be whole cookies; these are the bottom halves. Place the cookies 1 inch apart on the prepared baking sheets. Two baking sheets may be baked at the same time if they are placed on separate racks. Halfway through the baking process, the pans must be switched from one rack to the other and rotated 180° for even baking.

6. Bake for 7 to 9 minutes, or until the edges are brown. Cool for 2 minutes on the baking sheets, then transfer the cookies to a cooling rack. Cool completely.

7. Lay out a piece of wax paper on a work surface. Place the top cookie halves on the wax paper and sift confectioners' sugar over them.

8. On each bottom cookie half, spread 1 teaspoon of cranberry-orange relish. Top them with the top halves. Store in an airtight container at room temperature. They will begin to soften after a couple of days.

VARIATION: To make your own relish, in a colander, rinse 1 orange and a 12-ounce package of fresh cranberries. Don't peel the orange, but slice it in several wedges and remove any seeds. Place the slices in a food processor. Add the cranberries and ¾ cup sugar. Process until the orange is broken down into small pieces. (You may have to stop the processor to reposition an orange peel.) This will keep up to 1 week in an airtight container in the refrigerator or up to 3 months in the freezer. For this recipe, use ¼ cup plus 1 tablespoon, and use a mesh strainer to strain off any excess liquid.

STORAGE TIP: The dough can be frozen up to 3 months. Wrap it in plastic wrap and place it in an airtight container. Defrost in the refrigerator.

Hot Chocolate Cookie Cups

Makes 2 dozen cookies

PREP TIME: 45 minutes | **COOK TIME:** 20 minutes

Molded Cookies

The "cup" is a lightly flavored coffee cookie. The "handles" are made with pretzels. The "hot chocolate" is chocolate ganache. Place a plate of these on your holiday buffet table and it'll be empty in no time!

Cooking spray

2 cups flour

2 teaspoons espresso powder

½ teaspoon baking powder

½ teaspoon salt

8 tablespoons salted butter, at room temperature

½ cup firmly packed light brown sugar

½ cup granulated sugar

1 large egg

2 tablespoons plus 1 teaspoon plus 1 cup heavy cream, divided

1 teaspoon vanilla extract

2 cups semisweet chocolate chips

¼ cup white chocolate chips

½ teaspoon vegetable oil

24 mini pretzels, broken into pieces that resemble cup handles

36 mini marshmallows, halved

2 tablespoons chocolate jimmies

1. Preheat the oven to 350°F. Lightly coat a mini-muffin tin with cooking spray. Set aside.

2. In a medium bowl, using a wire whisk, combine the flour, espresso powder, baking powder, and salt. In a large bowl, cream the butter, brown sugar, and granulated sugar together until light and fluffy. Stir in the egg, 2 tablespoons and 1 teaspoon of the cream, and the vanilla. Mix until combined. Spoon 2 tablespoons of cookie batter into each prepared muffin cup.

3. Bake for 15 to 17 minutes, or until the edges are lightly brown. As soon as they are removed from the oven, using a ¼-teaspoon measuring spoon, push the center down on each cookie cup. Use a knife to loosen the edges so removing the cups from the muffin tin will be easier. Cool completely in the pan.

4. Place the chocolate chips in a small bowl. In a glass measuring cup, heat the remaining 1 cup cream in the microwave for about 1 minute, or until you see little bubbles around the edges. Once the cream is hot but not boiling, pour it over the chocolate chips. Let it sit for 10 minutes, then stir the mixture until smooth.

> RECIPE CONTINUED

5. In a glass measuring cup, combine the white chocolate chips and the vegetable oil. Microwave for 30 seconds. Add another 10 seconds at a time, if necessary, until melted.

6. Use a butter knife to dab a bit of the melted white chocolate "glue" to attach 2 pretzel "handles" to each of the cookie cups. Hold the handles in place for a few seconds until secured. Once all of the cups have handles, use a teaspoon to put chocolate filling in each cup. Add 3 mini marshmallow halves on top of the chocolate. Finish by sprinkling a few chocolate jimmies over the marshmallows. Store in a single layer in an airtight container at room temperature for up to 1 week.

TECHNIQUE TIP: Keep a bowl of hot water nearby when cutting the mini marshmallows. Dip the knife in the hot water before cutting. It will keep the marshmallow from sticking to the knife.

Minty Chocolate Chip Cookies

Makes 2 dozen cookies

PREP TIME: 25 minutes | **COOK TIME:** 15 minutes

Drop Cookies, Freezer-Friendly

These are amazingly simple to make and they are the perfect pick-me-up after a long day of holiday shopping. You get that deep chocolate satisfaction with the bonus of minty breath.

1 cup plus
2 tablespoons flour

⅓ cup unsweetened
cocoa powder

½ teaspoon
baking powder

¼ teaspoon baking soda

½ teaspoon salt

8 tablespoons
salted butter, at
room temperature

1 cup firmly packed light
brown sugar

1 large egg

1 teaspoon
peppermint extract

1 (10-ounce) package
mint-flavored
baking chips (see
Resources, page 146)
or 2 (4.67-ounce)
packages Andes
Crème de Menthe
Thins, unwrapped and
coarsely chopped

1. Preheat the oven to 375°F. Line two baking sheets with parchment paper. Set aside.

2. In a medium bowl, using a wire whisk, combine the dry ingredients. Set aside. In a large bowl, cream the butter and brown sugar together until light and fluffy. Mix in the egg and peppermint extract until completely incorporated. Completely combine the dry and the wet ingredients. Stir in the mint chips.

3. Drop 1 rounded tablespoon of cookie dough at a time onto the prepared baking sheets, at least 2 inches apart. Two baking sheets may be baked at the same time if they are placed on separate racks. Halfway through the baking process, the baking sheets must be switched from one rack to the other and rotated 180° for even baking.

4. Bake for 12 to 14 minutes, or until the cookies look firm. Cool for at least 2 minutes on the baking sheet, then transfer the cookies to a cooling rack. Cool completely. Store in a cookie jar at room temperature for up to 1 week.

INGREDIENT TIP: There are many mint-chocolate candy options on the market. I prefer Andes. It has a good-tasting chocolate and the mint isn't overwhelming.

STORAGE TIP: The baked cookies can be frozen for up to 3 months in an airtight container.

Santa's Toy Chest Cookies

Makes 12 dozen cookies

PREP TIME: 25 minutes | **COOK TIME:** 15 minutes

Drop Cookies, Freezer-Friendly

I get compliments on these cookies each and every time I serve them. People seem to like the different flavors and textures. I like them for two reasons: First of all, the recipe makes a ton of cookies, ideal for cookie exchanges, gift giving, and freezing part of the dough for later. Second, I get to pull out whatever is left in my baking pantry. Don't consider just chocolate chips; think about your cereals and protein bars. My most-complimented batch was made with butterscotch chips, dark chocolate chips, and leftover Post Great Grains Crunchy Pecan cereal. Just be careful about the combinations. I don't believe minty treats go that well with caramel ones. Once I've exhausted all of the leftover add-ins, I get to buy new ingredients to replenish my stores!

3⅓ cups flour

1 teaspoon salt

1 teaspoon cream of tartar

1 teaspoon baking soda

2 cups (4 sticks) salted butter, at room temperature

1 cup granulated sugar

1 cup firmly packed light brown sugar

4 large eggs

1 tablespoon vanilla extract

6 cups add-ins, such as semisweet chocolate chips, white chocolate chips, butterscotch chips, old-fashioned oats, unsweetened cereals, flaked coconut, raisins, chopped toasted nuts, and chopped candy bars

1. Preheat the oven to 350°F. Line two baking sheets with parchment paper. Set aside.

2. In a medium bowl, using a wire whisk, combine the flour, salt, cream of tartar, and baking soda. Set aside. In a large bowl, cream the butter, granulated sugar, and brown sugar together. Add the eggs one at a time, mixing after each addition. Mix in the vanilla. Add the flour mixture ¼ cup at a time until the dough is well mixed. Hand-stir in whatever add-ins you are using.

3. Drop 1 tablespoon of cookie dough at a time onto the prepared baking sheets, 2 inches apart. Refrigerate the remaining dough. Two baking sheets may be baked at the same time if they are placed on separate racks. Halfway through the baking process, the pans must be switched from one rack to the other and rotated 180° for even baking.

> RECIPE CONTINUED

4. Bake for 11 to 13 minutes, or until browned. Cool for 2 minutes on the baking sheet, then transfer to a cooling rack. Cool completely. Repeat with the remaining dough. For crispy cookies, store them in a cookie jar with a loose lid. For soft cookies, store them in an airtight container. Crispy or soft, the cookies keep for up to 1 week at room temperature.

INGREDIENT TIP: You can make even more interesting cookies if you save leftover chocolate-based Halloween candy. Place the wrapped candies in an airtight container in the freezer. On the day you make the cookies, unwrap the pieces one at a time, but don't defrost them. It is so much easier to cut the candy into pieces when it's still frozen. The cookies will be fine even if the candy is still a bit frozen. Valentine's candy works, too.

SERVING TIP: Make them twice the size by using a ¼-cup measuring cup to scoop out the dough. Place the completely cooked cookies in a decorative sandwich bag for gifting.

STORAGE TIP: The baked cookies and the dough both freeze beautifully in an airtight container for up to 3 months. Defrost in the refrigerator.

Red Velvet Crinkles

Makes 3 dozen cookies

PREP TIME: 30 minutes, plus 3 hours to chill | **COOK TIME:** 15 minutes

Freezer-Friendly, Molded Cookies

Just say the words *red velvet* and instantly the mind goes to an elegant cake being served for a special occasion. Red Velvet Crinkles are a close cousin. These beautiful, dark-red chocolate cookies are covered with snowlike clouds of confectioners' sugar instead of the traditional cream cheese frosting. Just the red in these cookies alone makes them a Christmas favorite.

2 cups flour

¾ cup granulated sugar

⅓ cup unsweetened cocoa powder

2 teaspoons baking powder

½ teaspoon salt

8 tablespoons salted butter, melted and cooled

4 large eggs, lightly beaten

2 teaspoons vanilla extract

1½ teaspoons red food coloring or ½ teaspoon red gel food coloring

1 cup confectioners' sugar

STORAGE TIP: The baked cookies will keep for up to 3 months frozen in an airtight container.

1. In a large bowl, using a wire whisk, combine the flour, granulated sugar, cocoa, baking powder, and salt. Stir in the melted butter, eggs, vanilla, and food coloring. Don't overmix.

2. Refrigerate at least 3 hours or up to 24 hours.

3. Preheat the oven to 350°F. Line two baking sheets with parchment paper. Set aside.

4. Sift the confectioners' sugar into a low-sided bowl. Shape 1 tablespoon of dough into a ball. Drop the ball into the confectioners' sugar. Roll it around until it is completely covered. Place the ball onto a prepared baking sheet. Repeat until both baking sheets are full. Refrigerate any remaining dough. Two baking sheets may be baked at the same time if they are placed on separate racks. Halfway through the baking process, the baking sheets must be switched from one rack to the other and rotated 180° for even baking.

5. Bake for 10 to 12 minutes, or until the top is almost firm. Cool for 2 minutes on the baking sheets, then transfer the cookies to a cooling rack. Cool completely. Repeat with the remaining dough. Store in an airtight container at room temperature for up to 1 week.

Candy Cane Cookies

Makes 20 cookies

PREP TIME: 30 minutes, plus 1 hour to chill | **COOK TIME:** 15 minutes

Freezer-Friendly, Molded Cookies

I made these when I first started baking Christmas cookies. I remember it being not much different than twisting two types of Play-Doh together. I hope you enjoy this updated version with a peppermint glaze sprinkled with crushed peppermints.

FOR THE COOKIES

2½ cups flour

1 teaspoon baking powder

½ teaspoon salt

1 cup (2 sticks) salted butter, at room temperature

1 cup confectioners' sugar, sifted

1 large egg

¼ teaspoon peppermint extract

¾ teaspoon red food coloring or red gel food coloring

FOR THE GLAZE

1 cup confectioners' sugar, sifted

1 tablespoon plus 1 teaspoon milk

1 teaspoon peppermint extract

4 candy canes or 8 red-and-white peppermint candies

TO MAKE THE COOKIES

1. In a small bowl, using a wire whisk, combine the flour, baking powder, and salt. Set aside. In a large bowl, cream the butter and confectioners' sugar together until light and fluffy. Mix in the egg until combined. Add the peppermint extract and combine well.

2. Divide the dough in half. Remove one half from the bowl, form it into a ball, and flatten it slightly. Wrap it in plastic wrap and refrigerate it. Add the food coloring to the other half in the bowl and mix well to combine. Form the red dough into a ball and flatten it slightly. Wrap it in plastic wrap and refrigerate for at least 1 hour or up to 24 hours.

3. Preheat the oven to 375°F. Line two baking sheets with parchment paper. Set aside.

4. Pinch off 1 tablespoon of the red dough and form it into a 5-inch rope. Repeat with 1 tablespoon of the uncolored dough. Twist the ropes together from top to bottom and curve the top to look like a candy cane. Place on a prepared baking sheet. Repeat for the remaining

> RECIPE CONTINUED

dough. Two baking sheets may be baked at the same time if they are placed on separate racks. Halfway through the baking process, the baking sheets must be switched from one rack to the other and rotated 180° for even baking.

5. Bake for 10 to 12 minutes, or until the edges are golden brown. Cool the cookies for 2 minutes on the baking sheets.

TO MAKE THE GLAZE

6. In a medium bowl, combine the confectioners' sugar, milk, and peppermint extract. Set aside. Place the peppermints in a heavy plastic bag and crush with a rolling pin.

7. Using a small spoon, drizzle the glaze over the cookies. Using your hands, sprinkle the crushed peppermints on the glazed portions of the cookies. Transfer the cookies to a cooling rack to cool completely. These cookies will last up to 1 week in an airtight container with parchment paper between each layer.

STORAGE TIP: The baked, unglazed cookies and the dough can be frozen for up to 3 months in an airtight container. Defrost in the refrigerator.

TECHNIQUE TIP: I enjoy the ease of food coloring, but gels offer more vibrant colors. To use them, push a toothpick into the gel, then dip the toothpick into the frosting and/or dough. Stir it around a bit, then finish up with the mixer. I use a new toothpick each time I add more gel until I get the desired color.

Chocolate Wedding Cookies

Makes 2 dozen cookies

PREP TIME: 30 minutes, plus 30 minutes to chill | **COOK TIME:** 15 minutes

Contains Nuts, Freezer-Friendly, Molded Cookies

Sprinkle a few of these along with Snowballs (page 49) on your next Christmas cookie board for contrast. Besides flavor, the difference between them is texture—they are rolled in granulated sugar, not confectioners' sugar, which lends a nice crunch. You can certainly use confectioners' sugar instead, if you like; if you do, roll them a second time in the confectioners' sugar after baking.

⅓ cup semisweet chocolate chips

1 tablespoon milk

2 cups flour

½ teaspoon salt

12 tablespoons salted butter, at room temperature

½ cup sugar, plus 2 tablespoons for rolling

2 teaspoons vanilla extract

½ cup chopped lightly toasted pecans (optional)

1. In a microwave-safe bowl, combine the chocolate chips and milk. Microwave for 30 seconds. Stir. If there are still whole chips, microwave for another 10 seconds. Stir again. Add another 5 seconds at a time, if needed, until the chocolate is fully melted. Set aside.

2. In a medium bowl, using a wire whisk, mix the flour and salt. Set aside. In a large bowl, cream the butter and ½ cup of sugar together until light and fluffy. Mix in the vanilla and melted chocolate until combined. Add the flour mixture, ¼ cup at a time, mixing after each addition, until combined. Hand-stir in the pecans, if using.

3. Chill the dough for at least 30 minutes or up to 24 hours.

4. Preheat the oven to 350°F. Line two baking sheets with parchment paper. Set aside.

> RECIPE CONTINUED

5. Put the remaining 2 tablespoons of sugar in a low-sided bowl. Shape the dough into 1½-inch balls. Roll the balls in the sugar until they are well covered. Place the sugared balls on the prepared baking sheets. Two baking sheets may be baked at the same time if they are placed on separate racks. Halfway through the baking process, the baking sheets must be switched from one rack to the other and rotated 180° for even baking.

6. Bake for 12 to 15 minutes, or until they are no longer wet looking. Cool for 2 to 3 minutes on the baking sheets, then transfer the cookies to a cooling rack. Cool completely. Store in an airtight container at room temperature for up to 1 week.

STORAGE TIP: The baked cookies and the dough will keep in the freezer up to 3 months. Freeze the cookies on a baking sheet overnight, then transfer to an airtight container. Wrap the dough in plastic wrap and place in a freezer bag; defrost in the refrigerator.

Mrs. Claus's Thumbprint Cookies

Makes 42 cookies

PREP TIME: 45 minutes, plus 1 hour to chill | **COOK TIME:** 15 minutes

Molded Cookies

Who is "Mrs. Claus" in your house? In our house, Mrs. Claus's favorite colors are red and green, making these one of her favorite Christmas cookies. She likes to roll the bottoms in green sugar and fill the hole with red jam. She also will use green jelly in a cookie rolled in red sugar. Now, Santa Claus is not quite so color-coordinated. He prefers the red jam in a cookie that has been rolled in regular granulated or raw sugar. It's up to you to choose which colors or jam flavors to go with.

2 cups flour

¼ teaspoon salt

1 cup (2 sticks)
   salted butter, at
   room temperature

¾ cup granulated sugar

2 large eggs, separated

1 teaspoon vanilla extract

Cooking spray

White, red, and/or green
   colored sugar

½ cup strawberry jam or
   mint jelly
   (or ¼ cup of each)

VARIATION: Any jam or jelly can be used; so can chocolate or pie filling. My favorite thumbprint cookies are rolled in almonds and filled with lemon curd. If you decide to make this variation, you'll need 1½ cups finely chopped lightly toasted almonds.

1. In a medium bowl, using a wire whisk, combine the flour and salt. Set aside. In a large bowl, cream the butter and granulated sugar together until light and fluffy. Mix in the egg yolks and vanilla until combined. Slowly add the flour mixture to the butter mixture. Mix until completely combined.

2. Cover the dough bowl with plastic wrap and refrigerate for at least 1 hour or up to 24 hours. Place the egg whites in an airtight container and refrigerate.

3. Preheat the oven to 350°F. Coat two baking sheets with cooking spray and wipe off any excess. Set aside.

4. Pour each colored sugar into a low-sided bowl. Lightly beat the egg whites and pour into a separate low-sided bowl.

> RECIPE CONTINUED

5. Roll the dough into 1½-inch balls. Dip each dough ball into the egg whites and then into the bowl of the colored sugar of your choice. Place the cookies on the prepared baking sheets 2 inches apart. Use your thumb to make an indentation in each of the cookies. Two baking sheets may be baked at the same time if they are placed on separate racks. Halfway through the baking process, the baking sheets must be switched from one rack to the other and rotated 180° for even baking. Bake for 15 minutes, or until the edges are light brown.

6. Meanwhile, put the jam in a small microwave-safe bowl. Microwave for 30 to 60 seconds and stir. This will loosen up the jam, making it easier to spoon into the cookies.

7. Cool the cookies for 2 minutes on the baking sheets, then transfer them to a cooling rack. As soon as they are slightly cool, press the centers again with your thumb.

8. Fill each center with jam (it'll be about ¼ teaspoon; no need to measure, you'll know the right amount). Store these cookies in an airtight container at room temperature for up to 1 week.

STORAGE TIP: The dough will keep for up to 3 months in an airtight container in the freezer. Defrost in the refrigerator.

Smooth Irish Whiskey Brownies

Makes 2 dozen brownies

PREP TIME: 30 minutes | **COOK TIME:** 30 minutes

Bar Cookie, Freezer-Friendly

Everyone has one friend who will say yes to almost any request. This is what I make for my special friend to say "thank you." Mind you, she's not a drinker, but she really loves these brownies. At first, she got them only for her birthday, but now I may make them for Christmas, too. Since they've become so popular with some of our other friends, these brownies have been making the rounds as holiday gifts. I don't always give an entire pan away; I may make it in two smaller pans.

FOR THE BROWNIES

Cooking spray

2½ cups granulated sugar

1½ cups flour

1 cup unsweetened cocoa powder

½ teaspoon salt

4 large eggs

1 cup (2 sticks) salted butter, melted and cooled

1 tablespoon vanilla extract

¼ cup Irish whiskey

FOR THE FROSTING

2 cups confectioners' sugar, sifted

1 cup (2 sticks) salted butter, at room temperature

3 tablespoons Baileys Irish Cream liqueur

1 cup semisweet chocolate chips

1 tablespoon coconut oil or vegetable shortening

TO MAKE THE BROWNIES

1. Preheat the oven to 350°F. Lightly coat a 9-by-13-inch baking pan with cooking spray. Set aside.

2. In a large bowl, using a wire whisk, combine the granulated sugar, flour, cocoa, and salt. Using a wooden spoon, stir in the eggs one at a time, mixing after each addition. Next, stir in the melted butter and vanilla. Pour the brownie batter into the prepared pan.

3. Bake the brownies for 26 to 30 minutes, or until a toothpick inserted in the center comes out clean. Carefully pour the Irish whiskey over the top. It will sizzle. Cool completely in the pan on a cooling rack.

TO MAKE THE FROSTING

4. In a large bowl, using an electric mixer, combine the confectioners' sugar, butter, and Baileys Irish Cream and beat until smooth. Frost the cooled brownies and place them in the refrigerator.

> RECIPE CONTINUED

5. Place the chocolate chips and coconut oil in a microwave-safe bowl. Microwave on high for 1 minute. Stir. If the chips have not melted, microwave for another 20 seconds. Drizzle the melted chocolate over the top of the brownies. Stored in the refrigerator in an airtight container, these brownies keep for up to 1 week.

STORAGE TIP: To freeze the entire pan of frosted brownies, wrap the top of the pan with plastic wrap or aluminum foil and place the pan in a resealable container. Individual brownies need be frozen overnight on a baking sheet, unwrapped. The next day, transfer them to an airtight container. They will keep for up to 3 months.

SUBSTITUTION TIP: You may substitute a box of store-bought brownie mix for the brownie batter ingredients. Prepare them according to the directions on the box. Pour the Irish whiskey over the top as stated in these recipe directions. No one will ever know the difference.

Colorful Candied Window Cookies

Makes 2 dozen cookies

PREP TIME: 45 minutes, plus 30 minutes to chill | **COOK TIME:** 10 minutes

Freezer-Friendly, Rolled Cookies

These beautiful treats—also known as stained-glass cookies—are a blast from my Christmas cookie–baking past. Back then, it was even more fun making them with my mother's help and seeing them baked than it was eating them. Make some memories and try baking these cookies with a loved one. Be sure to save the prettiest ones as ornaments to hang on your tree.

2¾ cups flour, plus ¼ cup for dusting

¾ teaspoon baking powder

¼ teaspoon baking soda

¼ teaspoon salt

1 cup (2 sticks) salted butter, at room temperature

1½ cups sugar

2 large eggs

2 teaspoons vanilla extract

20 to 40 pieces hard candy, depending on size (see Ingredient tip)

1. In a medium bowl, using a wire whisk, combine 2¾ cups of flour, the baking powder, baking soda, and salt. Set aside. In a large bowl, cream the butter and sugar together until light and fluffy. Add the eggs, one at a time, mixing after each addition. Mix in the vanilla. Add the flour, ¼ cup at a time, until the dough is well mixed.

2. Form the dough into a large ball, divide it in half, and wrap each half in plastic. Press them into 3-inch-tall disks. Refrigerate for at least 30 minutes or up to 24 hours.

3. Place the hard candies into separate heavy-duty freezer bags according to color, and seal the bags. Use the flat side of a meat mallet or roll with a rolling pin to crush the candies. Crush them as fine as possible. If the bags end up with holes, dump the crushed candy into individual bowls.

4. Place the remaining ¼ cup of flour in a low-sided bowl large enough for cookie cutters to fit in it. Flour your work surface and dust the rolling pin.

5. Preheat the oven to 375°F. Line two baking sheets with parchment paper. Set aside.

> RECIPE CONTINUED

6. Remove 1 disk of dough from the refrigerator and roll it out to ¼ inch thick. Dip the cookie cutter into the bowl of flour and then into the dough to cut out about 12 cookies. Use a smaller cutter or a paring knife to cut out the center of each cookie to hold the crushed candy. If the cookies will become ornaments, use a toothpick or a straw to make a hole at the top of the cookies so they can be hung. (Note: Once on the tree, these last only a few days.) Add any remaining dough to the other disk in the refrigerator.

7. Using a metal spatula, place the cookies on one of the prepared baking sheets. Fill in each hole with the candies. Make sure there's a slight mound in the center. Try to keep the candy pieces inside the holes and not on the dough. For a marbled or tie-dyed effect, make a couple of cookies with two different-colored candies in a hole.

8. Bake for 9 to 10 minutes, or until light brown. While the first batch is baking, prepare another batch of cookies with the other disk of dough. It's best to bake these cookies one pan at a time. Once baked, cool for at least 10 minutes on the baking sheet to make sure the centers stay attached to the cookies, then transfer the cookies to a cooling rack. Cool completely. Store in airtight containers at room temperature for up to 1 week.

INGREDIENT TIP: There is a plethora of hard-candy flavors and colors available. I love Jolly Ranchers, but you have to watch the flavors—they're not all compatible. Life Savers are a good option too. Since they have a hole in them, you'll need twice as many candies.

STORAGE TIP: The dough will keep for up to 3 months in an airtight container in the freezer. Defrost in the refrigerator.

Double Mint Brownies

Makes 2 dozen brownies

PREP TIME: 35 minutes | **COOK TIME:** 30 minutes

Bar Cookies

This is the sweet treat that my daughter is known for. Whenever there's a special event, and especially around the Christmas holidays, she brings these brownies into the office. They are so simple to make, and you'll never forget the flavor.

Cooking spray

2 cups sugar

1 cup vegetable oil or melted and cooled butter

4 large eggs

6 tablespoons unsweetened cocoa powder

1½ cups flour

1 teaspoon salt

2 teaspoons peppermint extract

28 pieces Andes Crème de Menthe Thins

1. Preheat the oven to 350°F. Lightly coat a 9-by-13-inch baking pan with cooking spray. Set aside.

2. In a large bowl, using a wire whisk, combine the sugar and vegetable oil. Stir in the eggs, one at a time, mixing after each addition. Stir in the cocoa, then the flour and salt. Stir in the peppermint extract until the batter is well combined. Pour the batter into the prepared pan.

3. Bake for 30 minutes, or until a toothpick inserted in the center comes out clean. Try not to over-bake them. While the brownies are baking, unwrap the candies and set them aside.

4. As soon as the brownies are out of the oven, place the candies on top evenly and carefully. After a few minutes, use a butter knife to push the candies down just a bit to help speed the melting process. Once the candies melt, use a silicone spatula to spread them evenly over the top of the brownies. Place the baking pan on a cooling rack to cool. Loosely cover the top of the cooled pan with foil or plastic wrap.

5. Cut the brownies into 24 pieces once the candy topping is hardened. Store, covered with plastic wrap, for up to 1 week at room temperature.

INGREDIENT TIP: Shhh, don't tell, but more than once my daughter has substituted a store-bought fudgy brownie mix for the base.

TECHNIQUE TIP: Place the candies imprinted side up. They tend to melt faster that way.

CHAPTER FOUR

New Creations

In this chapter you'll find recipes that aren't quite what you might think of when you think of Christmas cookies. They've been tweaked to add a little extra interest and perhaps to fill other needs, as well. The perfect dessert pizza is made with a sugar cookie crust that offers endless decorating possibilities. You'll find traditional recipes made with nontraditional cookie ingredients, like brie and beer, while others have a bit of hot spice. As we all know, bacon isn't just for breakfast anymore, so why not in a Christmas cookie? And if you can't get your little ones to eat their veggies at dinner, they'll be none the wiser when you serve them up "Eat Your Vegetables" Christmas Cookies.

Bacon and Eggnog Cookies

Makes 2 dozen cookies

PREP TIME: 35 minutes | **COOK TIME:** 15 minutes
Drop Cookies

They say bacon is good in everything and these cookies sure are tasty. It's nice to have a little variety around the holidays. And it's fun to see the look of surprise on folks' faces when they've taken their first bite!

Cooking spray

2½ cups flour

1 teaspoon baking powder

1 teaspoon freshly grated nutmeg

12 tablespoons salted butter, at room temperature

1¼ cups sugar

1 large egg

1 teaspoon vanilla extract

½ cup eggnog

6 bacon slices, cooked until crisp, drained, and crumbled

TECHNIQUE TIP: To microwave bacon, sandwich the slices between paper towels: three sheets on the bottom and three on top. Place on a microwave-safe dish and microwave on high for 6 minutes. If not completely cooked, flip it over and microwave for another minute or two. Once crisp, transfer the bacon to a clean paper towel and use another to pat off any extra fat.

1. Preheat the oven to 350°F. Lightly coat two baking sheets with cooking spray. Set aside.

2. In a medium bowl, using a wire whisk, combine the flour, baking powder, and nutmeg. Set aside. In a large bowl, cream the butter and sugar together until light and fluffy. Mix in the egg and vanilla. Mix in the eggnog. Add the flour mixture ¼ cup at a time, combining well after each addition. Hand-stir in the bacon.

3. Drop 2 tablespoons of cookie dough at a time onto the prepared baking sheets, leaving 2 inches between cookies. Two baking sheets may be baked at the same time if they are placed on separate racks. Halfway through the baking process, the baking sheets must be switched from one rack to the other and rotated 180° for even baking.

4. Bake the cookies for 15 minutes, or until the edges of the cookies are brown. Cool for 2 minutes on the baking sheets, then transfer the cookies to a cooling rack. Cool completely. Store in an airtight container at room temperature for up to 3 days.

Sharp Cheddar Cheese Butter Cookies

Makes 4 dozen cookies

PREP TIME: 30 minutes, plus 15 minutes to chill | **COOK TIME:** 30 minutes

Freezer-Friendly, Molded Cookies

Instead of regular butter cookies, why not try something a little different to put on your Christmas cookie board or buffet? These are just the savory bite that everyone wants to cut all of the sweetness. After the first crunch, they melt in your mouth. One is never enough—people will ask for more, because they are so addictive.

1¾ cups flour

⅓ teaspoon salt

¼ teaspoon dry mustard

¼ teaspoon cayenne pepper

5 cups shredded sharp cheddar cheese, at room temperature

8 tablespoons salted butter, at room temperature

Cooking spray

1. In a small bowl, using a wire whisk, combine the flour, salt, dry mustard, and cayenne pepper. Set aside. In a large bowl, cream the cheese and butter together. Gradually add the flour mixture and combine completely. Allow the dough to rest for 10 to 15 minutes in refrigerator.

2. Preheat the oven to 350°F. Coat two baking sheets with cooking spray. Wipe off any excess oil.

3. Shape the dough into 2-inch balls and place them on the prepared baking sheets. Press them down with a glass or a cookie press dipped in flour. Two baking sheets may be baked at the same time if they are placed on separate racks. Halfway through the baking process, the baking sheets must be switched from one rack to the other and rotated 180° for even baking.

4. Bake for 20 to 30 minutes, or until lightly brown and crisp. Store in a tightly covered container at room temperature for up to 1 week.

INGREDIENT TIP: Since I started making these, the color has changed—these cookies used to be yellowish orange. Now everything is white; no more artificial coloring. My favorite cheddar is called "Seriously Sharp Cheddar Cheese," and it is very sharp.

STORAGE TIP: The baked cookies can be frozen between layers of wax paper in an airtight container for up to 3 months.

TECHNIQUE TIP: This recipe can also be used to make other shapes, like cheese straws. Place the dough in a cookie press or a piping bag with a star tip. Press or squeeze the dough out in long straws onto the prepared baking sheets. Mark the straws every 4 inches or so with a knife so you can later break them into individual pieces. Bake at 350°F for 20 minutes.

Brie and Fig Jam Thumbprint Cookies

Makes 2 dozen cookies

PREP TIME: 45 minutes, plus 1 hour to chill | **COOK TIME:** 25 minutes

Contains Nuts, Freezer-Friendly, Molded Cookies

These cookies seem almost like a fancy hors d'oeuvre. With that first bite, you'll immediately taste both sweetness and saltiness. Making a cookie with brie isn't very different than using cream cheese. Sadly, fig jam is often overlooked, but it sits right on the shelf with other jams, like strawberry and grape. Step out of the box and serve your Christmas guests something a little different.

1½ cups flour

½ teaspoon salt

12 tablespoons salted butter, at room temperature

½ cup sugar

2 large eggs, separated

¾ teaspoon vanilla extract

Cooking spray

1 cup chopped lightly salted pistachios

1 (12-ounce) wedge brie cheese

¾ cup fig preserves

1. In a medium bowl, using a whisk, combine the flour and salt. Set aside. In a large bowl, cream the butter and sugar together until light and fluffy. Mix in the egg yolks and vanilla until combined. Slowly add the flour mixture to the butter mixture until completely combined. Refrigerate the dough, as well as the egg whites, for at least 1 hour or up to overnight (but no longer than 24 hours).

2. Preheat the oven to 350°F. Coat a baking sheet with cooking spray and wipe off any excess. Set aside.

3. Put the pistachios in a low-sided bowl. In a separate low-sided bowl, lightly beat the egg whites.

4. Shape the dough into 1½-inch balls. Dip the balls into the egg whites and then into the bowl of nuts, until completely covered. Place the cookies on the prepared baking sheet, 2 inches apart. Use your thumb to put an indentation in each cookie.

5. Bake for 15 minutes.

6. Meanwhile, cut the brie into ½-inch cubes and set aside. Heat the fig preserves in a small microwave-safe bowl in the microwave for 30 seconds to 1 minute and stir. This will loosen up the preserves, making them easier to spoon into the cookies.

7. Cool the cookies for 2 minutes on the baking sheet. If needed, press down the centers again. Carefully place 1 piece of cheese in each indentation. Spoon ½ teaspoon of fig preserves on top of the cheese.

8. Bake for 7 more minutes, or until the cheese is melted. Feel free to serve these while they are still warm or at room temperature. Store the cookies in an airtight container in the refrigerator for up to 1 week. If desired, reheat before serving.

VARIATION: You're not limited to brie and fig jam in this recipe. Try sharp cheddar cheese and chunky apple butter, or mozzarella and strawberry jam.

German Beer Chocolate Cookies

Makes 1 dozen cookies

PREP TIME: 25 minutes | **COOK TIME:** 25 minutes

Contains Nuts, Drop Cookies, Freezer-Friendly

This interesting recipe appeals to beer connoisseurs, who will love the fact you used a *dunkel* (dark German beer) in the dough; German chocolate cake lovers will enjoy the coconut frosting that tops the cookies. The sweet and flavorful frosting balances the slight tartness of the cookie.

FOR THE COOKIES

Cooking spray

1 cup flour

½ cup unsweetened
  cocoa powder

1 teaspoon salt

½ teaspoon baking soda

8 tablespoons
  salted butter, at
  room temperature

¾ cup sugar

1 large egg

¼ cup dark German beer

FOR THE FROSTING

½ cup evaporated milk

½ cup sugar

1 large egg

4 tablespoons
  salted butter, at
  room temperature

½ teaspoon
  vanilla extract

¾ cup sweetened
  shredded coconut

½ cup chopped
  lightly toasted
  walnuts or pecans

TO MAKE THE COOKIES

1. Preheat the oven to 350°F. Lightly coat a baking sheet with cooking spray. Set aside.

2. In a medium bowl, using a wire whisk, combine the flour, cocoa, salt, and baking soda. Set aside. In a large bowl, cream the butter and sugar together until light and fluffy. Mix in the egg until combined. Completely mix in the beer. Add the flour mixture to the butter mixture a little at a time until well combined.

3. Drop 1 heaping tablespoon of dough at a time onto the prepared baking sheet, leaving 2 inches between cookies. Bake for 10 minutes, until slightly firm and fragrant. Cool for at least 2 minutes on the baking sheet, then transfer the cookies to a cooling rack. Cool completely before frosting them.

> RECIPE CONTINUED

TO MAKE THE FROSTING

4. In a medium saucepan, combine the evaporated milk, sugar, egg, butter, and vanilla. Stir over medium heat until well combined. Continue stirring until the mixture thickens, 10 to 12 minutes. Remove the saucepan from the heat and stir in the coconut and nuts.

5. Allow the frosting to cool for 30 minutes. Spread the frosting on the cookies 1 teaspoon at a time. Store the frosted cookies in an airtight container at room temperature for up to 1 week.

INGREDIENT TIP: It is easy to confuse evaporated milk with sweetened condensed milk. Evaporated milk has the consistency of cream and can be substituted for cream in recipes that don't require it to be whipped. Many companies make it, but PET and Nestlé Carnation are the best known. Sweetened condensed milk is extremely thick and very sweet. Eagle Brand is a widely available brand.

Baklava Cheesecake Bites

Makes 30 cookies

PREP TIME: 45 minutes, plus 6 hours to rest and 1 hour to chill | **COOK TIME:** 15 minutes
Contains Nuts

These will be a hit at your next Christmas party. Once your guests bite through the crunchy phyllo cup into the flavorful nuts and finish with the creaminess of the cheesecake, they won't stop going back for more. The beauty of these is that the cheesecake layer helps cut the sweetness of the honey, which is what people think about when they think about baklava. Don't let the preparation time discourage you. Each step is simple and very doable.

FOR THE SHELLS

30 frozen phyllo
   dough shells

1½ cups walnuts,
   pecans, or pistachios,
   lightly toasted

½ teaspoon
   ground cinnamon

2 tablespoons salted
   butter, melted

FOR THE SYRUP

½ cup sugar

¼ cup honey

⅓ cup water

1 tablespoon freshly
   squeezed lemon juice

4 whole cloves

FOR THE FILLING

¼ cup heavy cream

4 ounces cream cheese,
   at room temperature

¼ cup sugar

½ teaspoon
   vanilla extract

TO MAKE THE SHELLS

1. Preheat the oven to 350°F. Arrange the phyllo shells on a rimmed baking sheet. Set aside.

2. Place the nuts in a food processor and process until coarsely chopped. Add the cinnamon and butter and process a few more times to incorporate them into the nuts.

3. Spoon 1 teaspoon of nut mixture into each phyllo shell. Reserve the remaining nut mixture in an airtight container and store at room temperature; it will be used later in the recipe.

4. Bake the shells for 10 minutes, or until the edges are light brown.

TO MAKE THE SYRUP

5. In a medium pan over high heat, combine the sugar, honey, water, lemon juice, and cloves. Continue stirring until the sugar is dissolved, turn down the heat, and simmer for 5 minutes without stirring. Discard the cloves.

> RECIPE CONTINUED

6. Spoon 1 teaspoon of syrup over the nut mixture in each shell. Reserve the remaining syrup in an airtight container at room temperature to be used later. Let the shells rest in an airtight container at room temperature for at least 6 hours or up to 7 days.

TO MAKE THE FILLING

7. Whip the cream with an electric mixer until stiff peaks form. Refrigerate while making the next layer.

8. Cream the cream cheese with the sugar. Add the vanilla and beat until well combined. Fold the whipped cream into the cream cheese mixture until just combined.

9. Spoon 1 teaspoon of cream cheese mixture into each shell. Sprinkle with the reserved nuts. Drizzle a little of the reserved syrup over the top of each shell. Refrigerate for 1 hour before serving. Store these in the refrigerator in an airtight container for up to 1 week.

INGREDIENT TIP: You can toast nuts in the microwave. Place them on a microwave-safe dish and microwave on high for 1 minute. Depending on the wattage, it may take longer; add 30 seconds at a time if needed. They are done when they begin to smell good. Beware that the nuts will continue to darken after they have been toasted.

"Eat Your Vegetables" Christmas Cookies

Makes 30 cookies

PREP TIME: 25 minutes | **COOK TIME:** 15 minutes

Contains Nuts, Drop Cookies, Freezer-Friendly

These are made with zucchini and carrots. The zucchini doesn't impart a flavor, but the carrots add a natural sweetness. Vegetables never tasted so good!

2½ cups flour

2 teaspoons baking powder

¾ teaspoon salt

½ teaspoon baking soda

1½ teaspoon ground cinnamon

1 teaspoon freshly grated nutmeg

12 tablespoons salted butter, at room temperature

¾ cup sugar

1 large egg

1 teaspoon vanilla extract or lemon extract

1 cup shredded zucchini, excess water squeezed out

½ cup shredded carrots

½ cup dark chocolate chips (optional)

½ cup coarsely chopped lightly toasted walnuts (optional)

1. Preheat the oven to 350°F. Line two baking sheets with parchment paper. Set aside.

2. In a medium bowl, using a wire whisk, combine the flour, baking powder, salt, baking soda, cinnamon, and nutmeg. Set aside. In a large bowl, cream the butter and sugar together until light and fluffy. Add the egg and mix it in. Mix in the vanilla until combined. Hand-stir in the flour mixture until barely combined. Add the zucchini, carrots, chocolate chips (if using), and walnuts (if using). Stir until just combined; try to not overmix.

3. Measure out 2 tablespoons of dough at a time and place on the prepared baking sheets, 2 inches apart. Two baking sheets may be baked at the same time if they are placed on separate racks. Halfway through the baking process, the baking sheets must be switched from one rack to the other and rotated 180° for even baking.

4. Bake for 12 to 14 minutes. Cool for 2 minutes on the baking sheets, then transfer the cookies to a cooling rack. Cool completely. Store in an airtight container at room temperature for up to 1 week.

STORAGE TIP: The baked cookies can be frozen in an airtight container for up to 3 months.

Sriracha Chews

Makes 4 dozen chews

PREP TIME: 15 minutes, plus 1 hour to harden | **COOK TIME:** 2 minutes

Contains Nuts, Drop Cookies

This is a slightly spicy variation on the same old haystacks (or chews) that show up at nearly every Christmas party. Sriracha hot sauce originated in Thailand; here, I use sriracha seasoning, which is available from a number of spice companies. You won't feel the heat until after you've finished your bite—but don't worry, the spiciness doesn't linger.

1 cup lightly salted dry-roasted peanuts

1 cup canned chow mein noodles

1 cup dark chocolate chips

1 cup milk chocolate chips

1 tablespoon sriracha seasoning or cayenne pepper

1. Line a baking sheet with parchment paper. Set aside.

2. In a large bowl, mix together the peanuts and chow mein noodles.

3. Put the dark chocolate chips and milk chocolate chips in a microwave-safe bowl. Microwave for 30 seconds. Stir. If needed, add 10 seconds at a time, stirring in between, until smooth. Once melted, quickly stir in the sriracha seasoning. Add the chocolate-sriracha mixture to the peanut mixture and mix until well combined.

4. Drop 1 tablespoons of the mixture at a time onto the prepared baking sheet, then refrigerate for at least 1 hour to harden the cookies. Store in an airtight container in the refrigerator for up to 1 week.

TROUBLESHOOTING TIP: These cookies will melt if you live in a warm climate or have warm hands, so they should be refrigerated. Take them out a few minutes before you want to serve them, as they can be very hard straight out of the refrigerator—you don't want to break a tooth!

Spicy Chocolate Cookies

Makes 2 dozen cookies

PREP TIME: 25 minutes | **COOK TIME:** 15 minutes
Drop Cookies, Freezer-Friendly

You can never get too much chocolate, and these cookies prove that statement. They make the perfect pick-me-up, especially during the hectic holiday season. Anyone who likes food with a kick will love these. Their spiciness pairs especially well with a glass of ice-cold milk.

Cooking spray

2½ cups flour

½ cup unsweetened cocoa powder

¼ cup instant espresso powder

1 teaspoon ground cinnamon

¾ teaspoon baking soda

¾ teaspoon salt

½ teaspoon cayenne pepper

1 cup (2 sticks) salted butter, at room temperature

1½ cups firmly packed light brown sugar

2 large eggs

1 teaspoon vanilla extract

1 cup dark chocolate chips

1 cup milk chocolate chips

STORAGE TIP: The baked cookies can be frozen for up to 3 months in an airtight container.

1. Preheat the oven to 375°F. Coat two baking sheets with cooking spray. Set aside.

2. In a medium bowl, using a wire whisk, combine the flour, cocoa, espresso powder, cinnamon, baking soda, salt, and cayenne pepper. Set aside. In a large bowl, cream the butter and brown sugar together until light and fluffy. Add the eggs one at a time, mixing after each addition. Mix in the vanilla until well combined. Add the flour mixture ¼ cup at a time, mixing after each addition. Hand-stir in the dark chocolate chips and the milk chocolate chips.

3. Scoop 2 heaping tablespoons of dough at a time onto the prepared baking sheets, leaving 2 inches between cookies. Two baking sheets may be baked at the same time if they are placed on separate racks. Halfway through the baking process, the baking sheets must be switched from one rack to the other and rotated 180° for even baking.

4. Bake for 9 to 11 minutes, or until slightly darker in color. Cool for at least 2 minutes on the baking sheets, then transfer the cookies to a cooling rack. Cool completely. Store in an airtight container at room temperature for up to 1 week.

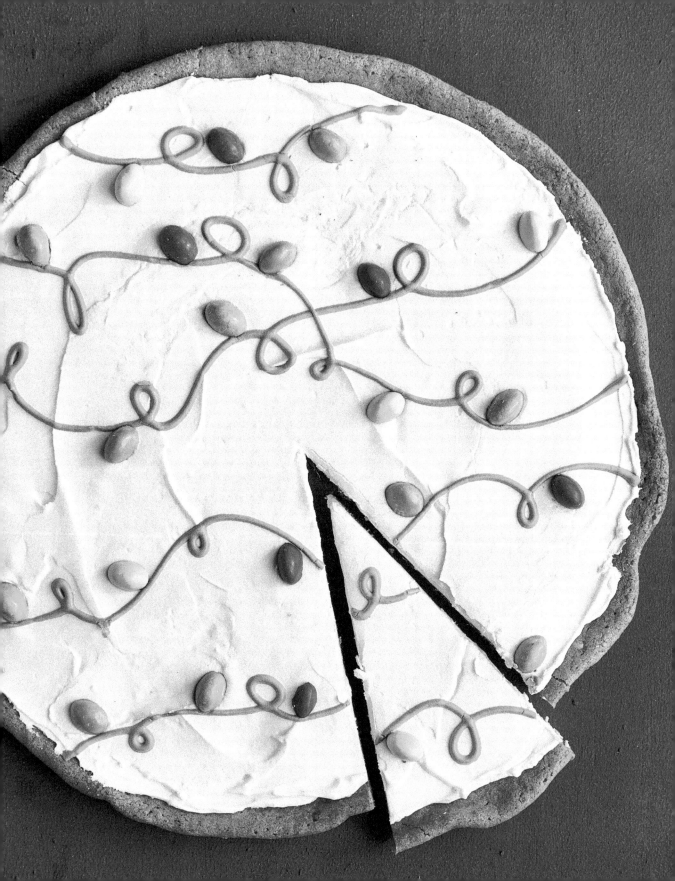

Christmas Cookie Pizza

Makes 6 to 8 pieces

PREP TIME: 25 minutes, plus 2 hours to cool | **COOK TIME:** 15 minutes

Freezer-Friendly, Molded Cookies

Let this be the focal point of your next holiday party. For an adult party activity, bake at least one cookie pizza per couple. Provide them with all kinds of edible decorations. For a kids' party, let them go wild with sprinkles, nonpareils, gummy bears, and other candies. Painting with icing is another option.

Cooking spray

1¼ cups flour

½ teaspoon baking soda

¼ teaspoon salt

8 tablespoons salted butter, at room temperature

¾ cup firmly packed light brown sugar

1 large egg

1 teaspoon vanilla extract

Royal Icing (page 7)

Green decorating gel

Multicolored candy-coated chocolates, cut in half

DECORATING TIP: There are so many ways to decorate this. Use red icing to represent tomato sauce and various candies and other edible items to help the cookie resemble an actual pizza. For a healthier option, ice the cookie with a cream cheese frosting and decorate with cut fruit.

1. Preheat the oven to 350°F. Lightly coat a baking sheet or a 12-inch pizza pan with cooking spray. Set aside.

2. In a medium bowl, using a wire whisk, combine the flour, baking soda, and salt. In a large bowl, cream the butter and brown sugar together until light and fluffy. Add the egg and mix it in. Stir in the vanilla. Add the flour ¼ cup at a time, mixing after each addition, until the dough is well mixed. Place the dough on the prepared baking sheet and shape it into a circle about 12 inches in diameter.

3. Bake for 15 minutes, or until the edges are brown. Cool the "pizza" on the baking sheet for at least 2 hours before decorating it.

4. Frost the top of the pizza with royal icing. Use green decorating gel to squirt out squiggly lines that resemble the wires of Christmas tree lights. Draw a couple of the wires so that the "lights" will hang off the side of the pizza. Place the candy halves every few inches apart just below, but touching, the green wires.

5. Cut into wedges for serving. Store in an airtight container at room temperature for up to 1 week.

Julekake Cookies

Makes 2 dozen cookies

PREP TIME: 30 minutes | **COOK TIME:** 40 minutes
Freezer-Friendly, Molded Cookies

Instead of eating fruitcake at Christmastime, I grew up with my father making *julekake*, a Norwegian bread loaded with candied fruit. I can still remember enjoying a freshly toasted piece with butter melting on top. I was never a big fruitcake fan, but I loved that bread. I also love these cookies. They take what's best about julekake—cardamom, candied cherries, and pineapple—and put them in bite-size form. Well, maybe two bites.

Cooking spray

2½ cups flour

¾ teaspoon
   baking powder

½ teaspoon salt

1 teaspoon
   ground cardamom

12 tablespoons
   salted butter, at
   room temperature

1 cup sugar

2 large eggs

1½ teaspoons
   vanilla extract

⅓ cup coarsely chopped
   candied pineapple

⅓ cup coarsely chopped
   candied red cherries

⅓ cup coarsely
   chopped candied
   green cherries (see
   Resources, page 146)

1. Preheat the oven to 350°F. Coat a baking sheet with cooking spray. Set aside.

2. In a medium bowl, using a wire whisk, combine the flour, baking powder, salt, and cardamom. Set aside. In a large bowl, cream the butter until fluffy. Slowly add in the sugar until combined. Add the eggs one at a time, mixing well after each addition, and then mix in the vanilla. Gradually add the flour mixture and combine completely. Hand-stir in the candied pineapple, red cherries, and green cherries.

3. Divide the dough in half and shape each into a 12-inch log. Place the logs on the prepared baking sheet. Flatten the tops until they are 1 inch tall. Bake for 30 minutes, or until the edges are light brown. Transfer the baking sheet to a cooling rack and cool for about 15 minutes.

4. Using a serrated knife, carefully cut the loaves into ½- to 1-inch slices. Place the slices cut-side down on the baking sheet. Bake for an additional 5 minutes, or until that side is light brown. Remove from oven and flip the cookies. Bake for another 5 minutes, or until the other side is light brown. Cool on the baking sheet for 2 minutes, then transfer the cookies to a cooling rack. Cool completely. Store in an airtight container at room temperature for 1 week.

STORAGE TIP: The baked cookies can be frozen in an airtight container, but once defrosted, they will be a little softer than freshly baked. Freezing the dough works wonderfully. Wrap the shaped logs in plastic wrap, then put them in a freezer-safe plastic bag or container. Defrost in the refrigerator. Both the cookies and the dough will keep frozen for up to 3 months.

TECHNIQUE TIP: To keep the candied fruit from sticking to your knife while cutting, dip the knife in cold water. If I have a lot of fruit to cut, I keep a small glass of cold water nearby.

Colorful Fruit Cookies

Makes 4 dozen cookies

PREP TIME: 25 minutes | **COOK TIME:** 10 minutes

Freezer-Friendly, Molded Cookies

These aren't just another colorful Christmas cookie. They have tasty, coordinating flavors that go with the colors. The gelatin you choose determines your cookie's flavor and color. Green gelatins come in lime and green apple flavoring; red gelatins come in strawberry, raspberry, and cherry flavors. Nothing says you can't make (blue) raspberry- and (yellow) lemon-flavored cookies instead of the red and green!

5 cups flour

2 teaspoons baking powder

2 teaspoons salt

1½ cups (3 sticks) salted butter, at room temperature

½ cup sugar, divided

4 large eggs

4 teaspoons vanilla or coordinating-flavored extract, half for each dough

1 (3-ounce) package green fruit-flavored gelatin mix

1 (3-ounce) package red fruit-flavored gelatin mix

1. In a medium bowl, using a wire whisk, combine the flour, baking powder, and salt. Set aside. In a large bowl, cream the butter and 1¼ cup of sugar together. Mix in the eggs one at a time and stir until completely combined. Add the flour mixture ¼ cup at a time until well combined.

2. Divide the dough in half. Using a dough hook in a stand mixer or using your hands, mix one half of the dough with the desired extract and dry green gelatin until fully colored. Place it in a separate bowl, cover with plastic wrap, and refrigerate. Repeat with the other half of the dough and the desired extract and dry red gelatin.

3. Preheat the oven to 325°F. Line two baking sheets with parchment paper. Set aside.

4. Put the remaining ¼ cup of sugar in a low-sided bowl. Shape the green dough into 1-inch balls. Dip the balls into the sugar and place them on the prepared baking sheets. Leave at least 1 inch between cookies. Press the cookies

> RECIPE CONTINUED

down with a fork to create a crisscross pattern (or use a cookie stamp with a seasonal design; see Resources, page 146). Repeat with the red cookie dough. Two baking sheets may be baked at the same time if they are placed on separate racks. Halfway through the baking process, the baking sheets must be switched from one rack to the other and rotated 180° for even baking.

5. Bake for 8 to 10 minutes, or until light brown around the edges. Cool for at least 2 minutes on the baking sheets, then transfer the cookies to a cooling rack. Cool completely. Store at room temperature for up to 1 week in a cookie jar with a loose lid for a crispy cookie or in an airtight container for a soft cookie.

INGREDIENT TIP: To enhance the chosen cookie flavors, use one of the various extracts available instead of vanilla. Don't substitute the sugar-free version of gelatin mix for the regular version—the cookies won't turn out right due to the different volumes. A regular gelatin box has 5 times the volume of the sugar-free version.

STORAGE TIP: The baked cookies or the dough can be frozen for up to 3 months in an airtight container. Defrost in the refrigerator.

TECHNIQUE TIP: If you use bare hands to mix in the dry gelatin, they may end up the same color as the cookie dough.

Christmas Cranberry Bars

Makes 2 dozen bars

PREP TIME: 40 minutes | **COOK TIME:** 25 minutes

Bar Cookie, Freezer-Friendly

These bars have a sweet-sour taste that many people enjoy. The cream cheese frosting puts these bar cookies over the top.

FOR THE BARS

Cooking spray

2¼ cups flour

1½ teaspoons baking powder

1 teaspoon ground ginger

¼ teaspoon salt

12 tablespoons salted butter, at room temperature

1½ cup firmly packed light brown sugar

2 large eggs

1 teaspoon vanilla extract

1 cup fresh cranberries

FOR THE FROSTING

4 tablespoons salted butter, at room temperature

¼ cup cream cheese, at room temperature

2 cups confectioners' sugar, sifted

1 teaspoon vanilla extract

TO MAKE THE BARS

1. Preheat the oven to 350°F. Coat a 9-by-13-inch baking pan with cooking spray. Set aside.

2. In a medium bowl, whisk the flour, baking powder, ginger, and salt. In a large bowl, cream the butter and brown sugar together until light and fluffy. Add the eggs one at a time, mixing after each addition. Mix in the vanilla. Add the flour mixture ¼ cup at a time until incorporated. Carefully stir in the cranberries so they don't break. Spread the dough into the prepared pan.

3. Bake for 18 to 21 minutes, or until light brown. Completely cool in the pan on a rack.

TO MAKE THE FROSTING

4. In a medium bowl, cream the butter and cream cheese. Add the confectioners' sugar ½ cup at a time, mixing until incorporated. Mix in the vanilla. Spread the frosting over the top of the uncut bars, then cut into 24 pieces. Refrigerate in an airtight container for up to 1 week.

STORAGE TIP: To freeze, place the cut bars still in the pan in the freezer overnight, then transfer the bars to an airtight container. They will keep up to 3 months.

CHAPTER FIVE

Not-Quite-Cookies

Not all handheld Christmas treats are flat, round, and made with flour, sugar, and butter. They're not all called cookies, either. Some Christmas treats are made with just nuts and chocolate. Some are closer to a cake than a cookie. And others might be made with cereal and popcorn. Some of the treats are bar cookies that are cut into rectangular or square serving pieces. Most of these recipes make great gifts, too.

Slow-Cooker Nutty Chocolate Clusters

Makes 3 dozen clusters

PREP TIME: 20 minutes, plus 2 hours to harden | **COOK TIME:** 3 hours

Contains Nuts

I can't remember a Christmas that I haven't made at least two batches of these. They make the perfect gift. I've given them in glass canning jars tied with a ribbon. I've placed them in insulated drinking glasses and in coffee mugs. I'll keep a few extra gift containers of them around just in case I need a last-minute gift.

2 (16-ounce) jars lightly salted dry-roasted peanuts

2 (24-ounce) bars white chocolate or milk chocolate almond bark, separated into squares

2¾ cups semisweet chocolate chips

TROUBLESHOOTING TIP: These are best made in a slow cooker that has only low and high settings. Fancier slow cookers that offer other settings often cook much faster than simpler models. These must be cooked on low. If you have a more advanced slow cooker, check the mixture after 2 hours. If the chocolate looks as if it is drying out, stir the mixture; it may be ready at this point.

1. Put the peanuts in a slow cooker. Add the pieces of almond bark. Top with the chocolate chips. Do not stir. Cook on low for 3 hours.

2. After cooking, unplug the slow cooker and allow the mixture to sit for 20 minutes.

3. While it cools, lay out a 3-foot-long piece of parchment paper on a level work surface.

4. Stir the mixture to ensure all of the nuts are covered in chocolate. Place the slow cooker insert on a trivet near your work surface. Using a long handled iced teaspoon, scoop out a heaping tea-spoonful of the chocolate-and-nut mixture onto the parchment paper. Continue until the slow cooker is empty.

5. Depending on your household humidity, it will take up to 2 hours for the clusters to harden. Store in an airtight container at room tempera-ture for up to 1 week.

VARIATION: Upgrade this recipe by using salted mixed nuts instead of peanuts and dark chocolate chips instead of semisweet chips. Another option is to make them with lightly salted toasted pecan halves—people go crazy for that option!

Polar Bear Chow

Makes 30 (½-cup) servings

PREP TIME: 20 minutes | **COOK TIME:** 5 minutes
Contains Nuts

One of the most desirable edible Christmas gifts are those that are sweet and salty. This treat fits the bill. This recipe makes enough to fill 10 wide-mouth, quart-size canning jars. Cover the lid with a square piece of holiday fabric, add a length of coordinating ribbon tied with a bow, and your gift is complete. Attach a label (I like to use blank business cards) with "Polar Bear Chow" on one side and your name on the other. If your friends have any food allergies, you may wish to list the ingredients, just in case.

6 cups Rice Chex cereal

3 cups red and green candy-coated chocolate pieces

3 cups mini pretzels

2 cups lightly salted mixed nuts

1 cup lightly salted dry-roasted peanuts

2 cups semisweet chocolate chips

1 cup creamy peanut butter

8 tablespoons salted butter

2 teaspoons vanilla extract

3 cups confectioners' sugar

1. In a very large bowl, combine the cereal, candy-coated chocolate, pretzels, mixed nuts, and peanuts. Set aside. Lay out a piece of wax paper big enough to hold all of the ingredients on a work surface.

2. In a heavy saucepan over medium heat, melt the chocolate chips, peanut butter, butter, and vanilla. Once melted, remove the pan from the heat. Cool for 3 minutes.

3. Slowly pour the chocolate mixture into the bowl with the cereal mixture, gently folding it in with a long-handled spoon.

4. Sprinkle the confectioners' sugar 1 cup at a time over the chocolate mixture, stirring constantly. Spread the mixture on the wax paper. Cool completely, then break into chunks. Store in an airtight container at room temperature for up to 2 weeks.

VARIATION: You don't have to use Rice Chex. Cheerios, Crispix, Life, Wheaties, and similar cereals work just as well. Avoid overly sweetened cereals; otherwise, your Polar Bear Chow will be too sweet.

Truffles

Make 6 dozen

PREP TIME: 20 minutes, plus 3 hours chill time | **COOK TIME:** 3 minutes

Molded

Truffles truly are opulent orbs of chocolate. What is so amazing is that they are very easy to make. These truffles are made with chocolate chips and sweetened condensed milk. Truffle centers may also be made from other food items like cookie crumbs. Leftover pound cake or angel food cake will work also. The best truffles are rolled by hand. If your hands tend to be warm, cool them off with cold water.

2 cups semisweet chocolate chips

1 cup dark chocolate chips

1 (14-ounce) can sweetened condensed milk

1 tablespoon vanilla or almond extract

Optional roll-ins and more: cocoa powder, powdered sugar, lightly toasted coconut, lightly toasted finely chopped almonds, nonpareils, sea salt

TECHNIQUE TIP: You can use a melon baller to shape them for consistency in size.

STORAGE TIP: Store in the refrigerator in an airtight container for up to 2 weeks. Before serving, allow them to sit out at room temperature for 15 minutes or so.

1. Combine chocolate chips and sweetened condensed milk in a microwave-safe bowl. Heat in the microwave for 2 minutes and stir. If needed, heat for another 30 seconds, which should fully melt the chips. Stir in the vanilla. Cover the bowl and refrigerate the mixture for at least 3 hours.

2. Line a jelly roll pan with parchment paper. Place roll-ins in low-sided bowl(s).

3. Shape the chocolate mixture into 1-inch balls. Roll them in the chosen ingredients. Chunky ingredients such as nuts should be lightly pressed down into the truffles. It's not necessary with powdered roll-ins like powdered sugar. Place them on the prepared jelly roll pan.

VARIATIONS: With all the roll-ins available to choose from, the flavor possibilities for these truffles are truly endless! You may even experiment with different spices. For a Spicy Mexican Coffee Truffle, omit the vanilla extract and instead add 1 tablespoon of strong coffee, 1/4 teaspoon ground cinnamon, and 1/8 cayenne pepper to the truffle mixture, then roll the truffles in cocoa powder.

Easy Cracker Bark

Makes 35 pieces

PREP TIME: 20 minutes | **COOK TIME:** 15 minutes

Contains Nuts

Here is another sweet-and-salty holiday snack. There is something so addictive about the flavor and texture combination of this bark that you can't stop eating it. Between Thanksgiving and New Year's, there's always a big pan of this sitting on a table in the back of my office. Once it's empty, a coworker will magically show up with another pan. She takes care of us during the holiday season.

Cooking spray

1 cup semisweet chocolate chips

1 cup dark chocolate chips

40 saltine crackers

1 cup (2 sticks) salted butter

1 cup firmly packed light brown sugar

1 cup sliced almonds, lightly toasted (optional)

VARIATION: Substitute 15 whole graham crackers for the saltine crackers. For either version, you can use the almonds or substitute chopped lightly toasted pecans and/or walnuts.

1. Preheat the oven to 350°F. Line a 10-by-15-inch jelly roll pan with aluminum foil and lightly coat it with cooking spray. Set aside.

2. In a small bowl, combine the semisweet and dark chocolate chips. Set aside. Fill the prepared pan with the crackers in a single layer. In a heavy saucepan, bring the butter and brown sugar to a boil and maintain for 3 minutes, stirring constantly. Carefully pour the butter-and-sugar mixture over the crackers. If necessary, use a silicone spatula to spread the mixture evenly.

3. Bake for 5 minutes, until the sugar mixture completely flattens out. Remove the pan from the oven and place on the stove top.

4. Sprinkle the chips over the sugary cracker layer. Wait about 5 minutes or so to allow the chips to soften. Once they are softened, spread the chocolate evenly. Immediately sprinkle on the sliced almonds (if using). Lightly press the almonds down into the chocolate.

5. Once the bark is cool, break it into 3- or 4-inch pieces. Store in an airtight container at room temperature for up to 1 week.

Ginny's Microwave Peanut Brittle

Makes 8 (½-cup) servings

PREP TIME: 10 minutes, plus 30 minutes to harden | **COOK TIME:** 10 minutes

Contains Nuts

Here is another signature holiday gift. My sister-in-law is well known for passing out this peanut brittle at Christmas. She gives tins to neighbors and brings one along when going to someone's house for dinner. It's become such a tradition that people almost count on it! This brittle is easy to make, and the best part is that you don't need a candy thermometer to get it right.

1 cup sugar

½ cup light corn syrup

1 cup lightly salted
  dry-roasted peanuts

2 tablespoons
  salted butter

1 teaspoon vanilla extract

1 teaspoon baking soda

TECHNIQUE TIP: For the glass bowl, I like to use my 2-quart glass measuring cup. It makes the mixture easy to pour.

VARIATION: I've also made this with salted cashews as well as salted mixed nuts. Both were very enjoyable.

1. Line a 12-by-17-inch jelly roll pan with parchment paper. Set aside.

2. In a large, glass, microwave-safe bowl, mix together the sugar and corn syrup. Microwave on high for 4 minutes.

3. Stir in the peanuts. Microwave on high for 3 minutes 30 seconds.

4. Carefully stir in the butter and vanilla. Microwave on high for 1 to 2 minutes.

5. Take the bowl out of the microwave and stir in the baking soda. This will cause the mixture to foam and bubble up. Quickly pour the mixture into the prepared jelly roll pan, spreading it out evenly. Place it on a cooling rack for at least 30 minutes.

6. Use your hands to break up the peanut brittle. Store in an airtight container at room temperature for up to 2 weeks.

Easy English-Style Toffee

Makes about 30 pieces

PREP TIME: 20 minutes | **COOK TIME:** 10 minutes

Contains Nuts

English toffee is featured in nearly every Christmas catalog that offers specialty foods. Made from butter, sugar, pecans, and chocolate, it is a deeply rich yearly indulgence.

1½ cups chopped lightly toasted pecans, divided

2 cups butter

2 cups sugar

2 cups semisweet chocolate chips

TECHNIQUE TIP: If you have a candy thermometer, the sugar mixture is cooked to the hard-crack stage, 295° to 309°F.

VARIATION: You can make this without the nuts, but the nuts are what make it so special. It's also nice with walnuts or almonds.

1. Line a 10-by-13-inch jelly roll pan with aluminum foil. Sprinkle ¾ cup of pecans in the pan. Set aside.

2. In a heavy saucepan over medium-high heat, melt the butter and sugar. While stirring continually, bring the mixture to a boil. The mixture with get bubbly and poof up slightly. After about 10 minutes, the sugar mixture will turn medium brown (very similar to the color of peanut butter). Once that happens, very carefully pour it over the pecans in the pan. Just as carefully, lightly tap the pan on the counter to remove any bubbles.

3. After 2 or 3 minutes, sprinkle the top of the toffee with the chocolate chips. Wait 5 minutes or so before using a silicone spatula to spread the melted chips evenly over the top. Sprinkle the remaining ¾ cup of pecans on top of the chocolate. Using a metal spatula or your fingers, press the nuts into the chocolate. Place the jelly roll pan on a cooling rack to speed the cooling process. Cool completely before breaking it into individual 3- to 4-inch pieces. Store in an airtight container in a cool place for up to 2 weeks.

Chocolate-Dipped Pretzel Rods

Makes 32 pretzels

PREP TIME: 30 minutes | **COOK TIME:** 1 minute

These are the perfect little holiday treat for those who don't care for sweets. The only limitation on decorating these pretzel rods is your imagination. For a simple version, dip the pretzels in milk chocolate, then drizzle white chocolate on top (or the other way around). I like to dip the rods into dark chocolate, then lightly roll them in sea salt.

Small edible decorations, such as mini candy-coated chocolates, sprinkles, toffee bits, finely chopped nuts, coconut, mini chocolate chips, and/or nonpareils of your choice

1 cup semisweet chocolate chips

2 tablespoons vegetable shortening, divided

1 cup white chocolate chips

32 pretzel rods

SERVING TIP: For gifting these, purchase tall, food-safe plastic bags made especially for food gifts. Tie a ribbon around the top to seal the bag. Or place three different decorated pretzel rods in a tall glass. For a formal dinner, place one at each table setting. They also make an excellent addition to a cookie board.

1. Set up an area for decorating the pretzel rods: Lay a 3-foot-long piece of parchment paper on your work surface. Set out the decorations in small bowls or in piles on the parchment. Reserve an area for two coffee mugs to hold the chocolate for dipping. Lay a 2-foot-long piece of parchment on another surface to place the decorated pretzel rods to set up.

2. Put the semisweet chocolate chips and 1 tablespoon of shortening in a heavy, tall coffee mug, and put the white chocolate chips and the remaining 1 tablespoon of shortening in another heavy, tall mug. Microwave for 30 seconds. Stir the chips. If they haven't melted, microwave for another 20 seconds. Stir. Add another 10 to 15 seconds at a time if needed until the chips are completely melted.

3. Transfer the mugs to your work surface. Dip a pretzel rod into one of the melted chocolates. Working quickly, sprinkle the chosen decorations on the rod. Place it on the other piece of parchment to set. Repeat with the rest of the pretzel rods. If the chocolate begins to harden, microwave it again for up to 20 seconds. When the decorated pretzels are set, store in an airtight container at room temperature for up to 1 week.

Flavorful Fruity Popcorn

Makes 16 (½-cup) servings

PREP TIME: 15 minutes | **COOK TIME:** 20 minutes

Having a holiday soirée? Place a few bowls of this popcorn around your house. Strawberry- and raspberry-flavored gelatins turn popcorn a pretty red, while lime and green apple gelatins yield an equally festive hue. As a Christmas gift, fill a tall, clear glass from the dollar store with popcorn. Stand the popcorn-filled glass in the center of a large piece of plastic wrap. Pull the four corners of plastic wrap up so they meet over the top of the glass and tie them together with a holiday bow. Besides holiday colors, think about taking this to your next team spirit party using your favorite team's colors.

8 cups popped butter-flavored microwave popcorn

4 tablespoons butter

3 tablespoons light corn syrup

½ cup firmly packed light brown sugar

1 (3-ounce) package flavored gelatin mix of your choice

15 drops red or green food coloring or up to ¼ teaspoon gel food coloring (optional)

TROUBLESHOOTING TIP: This recipe does not work with sugar-free gelatin. The sugar-free version is one-fifth the volume of regular gelatin.

1. Preheat the oven to 300°F. Line a rimmed baking sheet with aluminum foil or parchment paper.

2. Place the popcorn in a large bowl. In a medium saucepan over low heat, melt the butter and corn syrup, 3 to 4 minutes. Once melted, stir in the brown sugar and gelatin mix. Increase the heat and bring the mixture to a boil. Once boiling, turn the heat down to medium and stir in the food coloring (if using). Simmer for 5 minutes.

3. Pour the mixture over the popcorn. Using a long spoon, toss to evenly coat. Spread the colored popcorn in a single layer on the prepared baking sheet. Bake for 10 minutes; the popcorn will appear drier.

4. Transfer the baking sheet to a cooling rack. Once completely cool, break the popcorn into small pieces. Store in an airtight container at room temperature for up to 1 week.

INGREDIENT TIP: A bag of microwave popcorn makes about 12 cups. Do not use all of it. There won't be enough flavoring and coloring to cover it all.

Blondies

Makes 2 dozen blondies

PREP TIME: 20 minutes | **COOK TIME:** 30 minutes
Bar Cookies, Contains Nuts, Freezer-Friendly

Blondies have the same characteristics of brownies but without chocolate in the batter. It's a buttery bar cookie that offers multiple flavor options through the add-ins. I normally choose white chocolate and macadamia nuts, because they remind me of the time I spent in Hawaii. People are always blown away when given a tin of these decadent treats as a Christmas gift.

Cooking spray

2½ cups flour

¾ teaspoon baking powder

1 cup (2 sticks) salted
butter, melted
and cooled

1¾ cups firmly packed
light brown sugar

2 large eggs

2 teaspoons vanilla extract

1 cup chopped lightly
salted macadamia nuts

1 cup white chocolate chips

VARIATION: There are all kinds of alternatives to the macadamia nuts and white chocolate chips, including flavored chips, toffee pieces, coarsely chopped candies, dried fruits (like raisins), candy-coated chocolates, cereals, and nuts. If raw unsalted nuts are chosen, lightly toast them and add 1 teaspoon additional salt with the flour mixture.

1. Preheat the oven to 350°F. Lightly coat a 9-by-13-inch baking pan with cooking spray. Set aside.

2. In a large bowl, using a wire whisk, combine the flour and baking powder. Stir in the butter. Add the brown sugar and combine. Add the eggs one at a time, mixing after each addition. Stir in the vanilla and mix completely. Using a silicone spatula, stir in the macadamias and chocolate chips. Pour the batter into the prepared pan.

3. Bake for 25 to 30 minutes, or until a toothpick inserted in the center comes out clean. Place the baking pan on a cooling rack. Cool completely. Store, covered with plastic wrap, for up to 1 week at room temperature.

INGREDIENT TIP: Is white chocolate really chocolate? Technically, no. It is made with cocoa butter, sugar, and milk solids. It's missing the cocoa solids, which are what provides the flavor and dark color found in chocolate.

STORAGE TIP: Baked blondies cut into squares or the entire pan may be frozen in an airtight container for up to 3 months.

Raspberry Linzer Tortes

Makes 2 dozen tortes

PREP TIME: 25 minutes | **COOK TIME:** 40 minutes

Bar Cookies, Contains Nuts

These are a holiday classic, perfect served with a dollop of whipped cream. There is something so special when you first bite into the slightly crunchy crust and discover the deep raspberry flavor inside. It's hard to find a cookie swap that doesn't include them.

Salted butter, at
 room temperature,
 for greasing

2 cups flour

2 cups ground almonds
 (see Ingredient tip)

¾ cup sugar

1 teaspoon
 ground cinnamon

1½ cups (3 sticks) cold
 salted butter

1 cup seedless
 raspberry preserves,
 slightly warmed

STORAGE TIP: The baked tortes can be frozen for up to 3 months in an airtight container.

VARIATION: Add the grated zest of 1 lemon to the crust mixture, and substitute store-bought lemon curd for the raspberry preserves.

1. Preheat the oven to 350°F. Lightly grease a 9-by-13-inch baking pan with butter. Set aside.

2. In a large bowl, using a wooden spoon, combine the flour, ground almonds, sugar, and cinnamon.

3. Cut the cold butter into cubes. Use a pastry blender, two knives, or your hands to blend it into the flour mixture. The mixture should look like little peas and there shouldn't be patches of loose flour. Press 2 cups of the dough into the prepared pan. Spread the raspberry preserves over the top. Crumble the rest of the dough over the raspberry preserves. Gently press the topping into the preserves.

4. Bake for 35 to 40 minutes, or until the top is lightly brown. Cool the tortes in the pan on a cooling rack, then cut into bars. Store in an airtight container at room temperature for up to 1 week.

INGREDIENT TIP: Ground almonds (or almond meal) is not the same thing as almond flour, which is too finely ground to use in this recipe. To make your own, very coarsely chop 1¾ cups blanched almonds, then process about ½ cup at a time in a food processor until it has a grainy texture. Use within 2 days, as it can go rancid.

Crispy Holiday Trees

Makes 2 dozen trees

PREP TIME: 25 minutes | **COOK TIME:** 5 minutes
Bar Cookies

Who knew that a cereal would be turned into so many more things than breakfast? Once butter and melted marshmallows are added to rice cereal, you get crispy rice treats. Here they are turned into tree-shaped holiday treats, which not only taste good but are fun to decorate.

Salted butter, at room temperature, for greasing, plus 4 tablespoons

40 standard-size marshmallows or 4 cups mini marshmallows

6 cups crispy rice cereal

Royal Icing (page 7), in desired color(s)

Mini candy-coated chocolates and/or red and green nonpareils, for decorating

STORAGE TIP: Store the unfrosted trees in an airtight container until ready to decorate them.

1. Lightly butter a 9-by-13-inch baking pan.

2. In a large, heavy saucepan over medium-low heat, melt the remaining 4 tablespoons of butter, 3 to 4 minutes. Add the marshmallows and stir until completely melted. Remove from the heat. Using a large, buttered wooden spoon, quickly stir in the cereal until it is completely coated with the marshmallow mixture.

3. Pour the cereal mixture into the prepared pan. Using lightly greased wax paper, a buttered spatula, or your lightly buttered fingers, evenly press the mixture into all corners of the pan. For quicker cooling, place the pan on a cooling rack.

4. Once cool, cut into triangles. Begin by cutting it into 12 pieces (3 squares by 4 squares). Cut each in half diagonally for 24 triangles. To make larger trees, cut it into 6 pieces (2 squares by 3 squares), then cut in half for a total of 12 trees.

5. Frost with royal icing. Use either or both candy-coated chocolates and nonpareils as ornaments. Put a different-colored icing in a piping bag with a star tip to form the star at the top of the tree. Store in a single layer in an airtight container. They should be consumed within 24 hours as the icing will start to soften the cookies.

Dream of a White Christmas Bars

Makes 9 or 16 bars

PREP TIME: 20 minutes | **COOK TIME:** 40 minutes

Bar Cookies, Freezer-Friendly

Coconut fans, rejoice! This is for you. Be assured, you'll be dreaming of a white Christmas while eating one of these sweet and chewy bars. Most dream bars are made with chocolate and nuts, but not this recipe. Aside from the coconut, it's got the same crust as a pie, and it's prebaked to maximize the flavor of the pastry.

Cooking spray

1¼ cups flour, divided

1 cup firmly packed light brown sugar, divided

8 tablespoons cold salted butter

2 large eggs

1 teaspoon vanilla extract

½ teaspoon baking powder

¼ teaspoon salt

2¼ cups sweetened coconut flakes

INGREDIENT TIP: You could use unsweetened coconut instead, but be sure to add more sugar to the recipe before baking.

STORAGE TIP: These bars may be frozen up to 3 months in an airtight container.

1. Preheat the oven to 350°F. Lightly coat a 9- or 8-inch square baking pan with cooking spray.

2. In a large bowl, using a wire whisk, combine 1 cup of flour and ½ cup of brown sugar. Cut the butter into cubes. Use a pastry blender, two knives, or your hands to blend it into the flour mixture. The mixture should look like little peas and there shouldn't be patches of loose flour. Transfer the mixture to the prepared baking pan. Use your hands to press it evenly into the pan.

3. Bake for 15 minutes, or until the edges are golden brown.

4. Meanwhile, in a medium bowl, lightly whisk the eggs. Whisk in the vanilla. Using an electric mixer, blend in the remaining ¼ cup of flour, the remaining ½ cup of brown sugar, the baking powder, and salt. Hand-stir in the coconut flakes.

5. Let the crust cool for a few minutes, then add the coconut mixture on top.

6. Bake for 25 more minutes, or until the top is lightly brown. Place the baking pan on a cooling rack. Once the bars are cool, cut them into 9 or 16 pieces. Store in an airtight container at room temperature for up to 1 week.

Orange Snow Bars

Makes 9 bars

PREP TIME: 25 minutes | **COOK TIME:** 40 minutes

Bar Cookies

These are a nice change from all of the chocolate and other overly sweet items found during the Christmas season, with their fresh taste of citrus. They are pretty to look at, too. Serve them at holiday parties on a doily-lined tray or watch someone's face light up when they open up their very own tin.

FOR THE CRUST

Unsalted butter, at room temperature, for greasing

1 cup flour

¼ cup confectioners' sugar, sifted, plus more for dusting

8 tablespoons cold salted butter

FOR THE FILLING

2 large eggs

¾ cup granulated sugar

3 tablespoons orange juice

2 tablespoons flour

¼ teaspoon baking powder

1 tablespoon grated orange zest

VARIATION: Any citrus flavor will work with these bars. Try using key lime juice for a southern Florida summer vibe.

TO MAKE THE CRUST

1. Preheat the oven to 350°F. Lightly grease an 8- or 9-inch square baking pan with butter. Set aside.

2. In a large bowl, using a wire whisk, combine the flour and confectioners' sugar. Cut the cold butter into cubes. Using a pastry blender, two knives, or your hands, blend it into the flour mixture. The mixture should look like large peas. Pat the crust into the prepared pan.

3. Bake for 10 to 12 minutes, or until the edges are golden brown. Place the pan on a cooling rack.

TO MAKE THE FILLING

4. In a medium bowl, using an electric mixer, beat the eggs, granulated sugar, and orange juice until well combined. Mix in the flour and baking powder. Hand-stir in the orange zest. Pour the filling over the cooled crust.

5. Return the pan to the oven and bake for 20 to 25 minutes, or until the edges look firm.

6. Place the pan on a cooling rack. Sift confectioners' sugar over the top and cut into 9 bars. Store in an airtight container at room temperature for up to 1 week.

Red Velvet Cheesecake Bars

Makes 9 or 16 bars

PREP TIME: 35 minutes | **COOK TIME:** 40 minutes
Bar Cookies, Freezer-Friendly

Just one bite into one of these fudgy bars and you'll never want a regular brownie again. Since they are pretty, too, these bars are perfect for Christmas gift giving. Either place a few in a decorative tin or wrap one bar in a piece of plastic wrap and then place it in a resealable Christmas bag.

Salted butter, at
   room temperature,
   for greasing

¾ cup flour

¼ cup unsweetened
   cocoa powder

½ teaspoon baking soda

½ teaspoon salt

1¼ cups sugar, divided

½ cup vegetable oil or
   melted butter

3 large eggs, divided

2 teaspoons red
   food coloring

1 teaspoon white vinegar

1½ teaspoons vanilla
   extract, divided

1 (8-ounce) package
   cream cheese, at
   room temperature

INGREDIENT TIP: Why vinegar? It helps to set the red color in the bars; you won't taste it.

1. Preheat the oven to 350°F. Lightly grease an 8- or 9-inch square baking pan with butter.

2. In a large bowl, whisk the flour, cocoa, baking soda, and salt. Add 1 cup of sugar, the vegetable oil, 2 eggs, the food coloring, vinegar, and 1 teaspoon of vanilla. Stir until well combined. Pour the batter into the prepared pan.

3. In a medium bowl, cream the cream cheese and the remaining ¼ cup of sugar until light and fluffy. Mix in the last egg and remaining ½ teaspoon of vanilla.

4. Dollop rounded tablespoons of the cheesecake mixture over the top of the batter. Pull a knife through the two mixtures to create a swirl effect.

5. Bake for 30 to 37 minutes, or until a toothpick inserted in the center comes out clean. Place the pan on a cooling rack. Once cool, cut the bars into either 9 or 16 pieces, depending on whether you will give them as a gift or include them with other cookies to serve. Stored in an airtight container, these will keep for up to 1 week.

STORAGE TIP: These bars can be frozen in an airtight container for up to 3 months.

No-Bake Christmas Wreaths

Makes 20 wreaths

PREP TIME: 35 minutes | **COOK TIME:** 10 minutes

Molded Cookies

These really pretty Christmas wreaths have been around for a long as I can remember. This recipe makes just enough to decoratively space them around on your holiday cookie board.

8 tablespoons salted butter, at room temperature

1 (10-ounce) package marshmallows

1½ teaspoons green food coloring

5 cups corn flakes cereal

Red Hots and/or mini red candy-coated chocolates

TECHNIQUE TIP: To make these in the microwave, put the butter and marshmallows in a microwave-safe bowl and microwave on high for 1 minute. If they are not melted, microwave for 30 seconds more. Stir. If needed, add 10 seconds at a time until the butter and marshmallows stir together properly. Use a silicone spatula to add the melted butter and marshmallows to the cereal. You must work quickly so the cereal and marshmallow mixture properly combine.

1. Line a baking sheet with parchment paper. Set aside.

2. In a Dutch oven over medium heat, melt the butter. Add the marshmallows and stir until the marshmallows are melted. Stir in the food coloring.

3. Add the corn flakes to the marshmallow mixture. Stir until the cereal is completely green. Spoon out ¼ cup of the mixture onto the prepared baking sheet. Working quickly with buttered fingers, shape the mixture into a wreath. Decorate each wreath with the Red Hots and/or the candy-coated chocolates. Repeat until all of the wreaths are made.

4. Once set, store the wreaths between layers of parchment paper in an airtight container. They should keep their flavor and texture for at least 3 days.

No-Bake Chocolate Cookies

Makes 3 dozen cookies

PREP TIME: 15 minutes, plus 2 hours to harden | **COOK TIME:** 10 minutes

Molded Cookies, Contains Nuts

These no-bake cookies are known by several names, including "preacher cookies." According to legend, you could make these cookies faster than the preacher would make it up your front walk for a visit. During the Christmas season, friends may also stop by without calling ahead. It's a good idea to always have these ingredients on hand to throw together for unexpected holiday company.

8 tablespoons salted butter, at room temperature

2 cups sugar

¼ cup unsweetened cocoa powder

½ cup milk

½ cup peanut butter

1 teaspoon vanilla extract

3 cups old-fashioned oats

1. Line a baking sheet with parchment paper. Set aside.

2. In a large, heavy saucepan over medium-high heat, melt the butter. Add the sugar and cocoa and stir together. Add the milk and stir until well combined. Bring to a boil and maintain it for 2 minutes.

3. Remove the pan from the heat and stir in the peanut butter and vanilla. Add the oats and stir until they are completely covered with the chocolate mixture.

4. Drop the mixture 1 tablespoon at a time onto the prepared baking sheet. Place the sheet on a cooling rack and allow the cookies to harden for about 2 hours. To speed up the process, place them in the refrigerator. Store in an airtight container at room temperature for up to 1 week.

INGREDIENT TIP: Some recipes use quick-cooking oats instead of the old-fashioned oats. I prefer the texture of old-fashioned oats, but it's up to you. Old-fashioned oats hold their texture better, providing more chewiness. The amount is the same for either.

Measurement Conversions

	US STANDARD	US STANDARD (OUNCES)	METRIC (APPROXIMATE)
VOLUME EQUIVALENTS (LIQUID)	2 tablespoons	1 fl. oz.	30 mL
	¼ cup	2 fl. oz.	60 mL
	½ cup	4 fl. oz.	120 mL
	1 cup	8 fl. oz.	240 mL
	1½ cups	12 fl. oz.	355 mL
	2 cups or 1 pint	16 fl. oz.	475 mL
	4 cups or 1 quart	32 fl. oz.	1 L
	1 gallon	128 fl. oz.	4 L
VOLUME EQUIVALENTS (DRY)	⅛ teaspoon		0.5 mL
	¼ teaspoon		1 mL
	½ teaspoon		2 mL
	¾ teaspoon		4 mL
	1 teaspoon		5 mL
	1 tablespoon		15 mL
	¼ cup		59 mL
	⅓ cup		79 mL
	½ cup		118 mL
	⅔ cup		156 mL
	¾ cup		177 mL
	1 cup		235 mL
	2 cups or 1 pint		475 mL
	3 cups		700 mL
	4 cups or 1 quart		1 L
	½ gallon		2 L
	1 gallon		4 L
WEIGHT EQUIVALENTS	½ ounce		15 g
	1 ounce		30 g
	2 ounces		60 g
	4 ounces		115 g
	8 ounces		225 g
	12 ounces		340 g
	16 ounces or 1 pound		455 g

	FAHRENHEIT (F)	CELSIUS (C) (APPROXIMATE)
OVEN TEMPERATURES	250°F	120°C
	300°F	150°C
	325°F	180°C
	375°F	190°C
	400°F	200°C
	425°F	220°C
	450°F	230°C

Resources

THESE DAYS, JUST ABOUT ANYTHING CAN BE PURCHASED ONLINE. All that is required is typing the name of the desired product into a search engine and then just waiting for the results to pop up. Stores that carry cookie-making supplies range from local grocery stores and Walmart to craft stores, such as JOANN Fabrics and Crafts, Michaels, and Hobby Lobby. If you're lucky, you may have a cake-decorating or kitchen store nearby. They could be good resources, also. For equipment and gift-giving items, don't forget about thrift stores and local yard sales. Even if you don't have the time to go often, you must have one friend who does. That's probably the person in your life who lives for the hunt for a good deal. Also, before spending a bunch of money on an expensive piece of equipment, such as a stand mixer, see if you can borrow one from a friend. Take it for a test drive. You may realize it's not worth the money, or you may find out the one you wanted doesn't have a big-enough bowl.

Ingredients

The very best time to start shopping for Christmas cookie ingredients is around the end of October, which begins the 2½-month-long baking season. Special store displays will appear featuring all types of regular and specialty items found only at this time of year. Be sure to look at the sell-by, best-by, and/or use-by dates. Most sugary items will last in your panty for a couple of years. Use this time to purchase some of those items that you may not need until later in the year. If your pantry is crowded, create a list so you won't keep buying the same ingredients over and over.

FLOURS, SUGARS, BUTTER, EGGS, AND MORE

If you're baking a tremendous number of cookies, besides shopping at your local grocery store, don't forget the warehouse stores, such as Sam's Club, Costco Wholesale, and BJ's Wholesale Club for bulk bargains.

CINNAMON EXTRACT AND OTHER UNUSUAL EXTRACTS

These also show up right after Halloween and disappear when they are sold out, which is usually mid-January. Extracts can easily last for several years.

SPICES

If your local grocery store or specialty market doesn't have the spices you want, try looking online. Penzeys Spices has almost any spice available. Penzeys has some physical stores, but it also has an excellent online shop.

CRANBERRIES

Fresh cranberries are available in the United States from middle of September through the holiday season. They can be found in the produce section of your local grocery store. Be sure to freeze a few extra bags for later use. They'll still be good frozen for at least a year.

POPPY SEED, PLUM, AND RASPBERRY FILLINGS

Solo is the main company that makes these fillings. Typically, they can be found in your local market or in an upscale store, like The Fresh Market.

FIG JAM

Stonewall Kitchen is one of the companies that make fig jam. Its products can be found in some local grocery stores and in specialty stores.

CANDIED FRUITS

Candied fruits start showing up during the baking season. I usually pick mine up after Christmas for half the price. Most candied fruits can last for up to 2 years.

SPECIALTY CHIPS AND OTHER COOKIE ADD-INS

Mint chocolate chips, cinnamon chips, and more are usually found in the special area set up in the grocery store just for the baking season or in the regular baking aisle.

MERINGUE POWDER

Wilton makes this product specifically for use in baking. It can be found online as well as at Walmart and major craft stores.

ROYAL ICING

Yes, you can purchase royal icing. Wilton makes it, and it is sold online and in craft stores.

REGULAR ICING

Grocery stores, Walmart, and craft stores all carry already colored and flavored icings. It may be more convenient to purchase an already-colored icing, but it will never taste as good as homemade.

SPRINKLES, JIMMIES, SANDING SUGAR, CRYSTAL SUGAR, NONPAREILS (MINIATURE DECORATING CANDIES)

Most grocery stores carry at least colored sprinkles and chocolate jimmies in their baking aisle. For more extravagant items, such as seasonal sprinkles and colored sanding sugars, Walmart, craft stores, and kitchen shops are your best bet.

FOOD COLORING

McCormick is the biggest name in food coloring and egg dye. It can almost always be found in your local grocery store. During the baking season, you can buy single colors, but a box of the four primary colors may be purchased almost anytime. McCormick has a chart on its website that tells you how many drops of each color are necessary to make different colors.

ICING GELS

Local grocery stores are now starting to offer sets of primary icing colors. For a larger selection, Wilton makes at least 25 different-colored icing gels. They also have a chart on their website for making other colors. Wilton products are sold online, at Walmart, and in craft stores.

Equipment

Most cookies can be made with the equipment you already have in your kitchen. If you want to make specialized cookies or are just into kitchen "toys," here is where you can find most of the desired cookie-making equipment.

BAKING SHEETS

I've got too many baking sheets. The ones I use the most are the ones that I found at Sam's Club. They are 13-by-18-inch shiny metal pans with sides, and they are very sturdy. They are also called half sheet pans. Most recipes are written for shiny metal pans. Dark metal pans can cause the cookies to cook quicker. I'm not a fan of no-burn, double-layered cookie sheets, either; the cookies don't cook at the specified recipe times. Baking sheets can be found almost anywhere, from the local grocery store to Amazon.

COOKIE-DECORATING SUPPLIES (ROLLING PINS, PIPING BAGS, PIPING TIPS, COUPLERS, AND MORE)

Walmart and the major craft stores are a good source for these. Online, Amazon and Wilton also sell them.

ELECTRIC COOKIE PRESS

I've had my Salton Electric Cookie Press for many years. These days, the only Salton-brand ones I've seen are sold used on eBay and Amazon. You can purchase a new electric cookie press from Cuisinart.

COOKIE STAMPS

Cookie stamps come in several forms. The simplest version will stamp an image into a ball of dough while pressing it flat. Another type may cut the cookie dough while imprinting an image. Some cookie stamps come in a set that includes a cutter in a particular shape and then another piece used to cut a design in the cookie. Cookie stamps may be purchased online. Walmart and craft stores may also sell them. There are several people on Etsy that can design cookie stamps and cutters personalized just for the buyer.

COOKIE CUTTERS

They come in plastic and metal. Your local grocery store as well as Walmart may sell a simple set of cookie cutters. Craft stores and specialty kitchen shops sell them as well. The largest selection can be found online. American Tradition Cookie Cutters has a huge selection. I counted 74 Christmas cookie cutters alone. They can be purchased individually, and most of the cutters are less than $1 apiece.

COOKIE MOLDS

Traditional cookie molds are wooden and can be found in specialty kitchen shops and online. They come also in plastic.

EMBOSSED ROLLING PINS

A huge selection of embossed rolling pins can be found on Etsy. You may find them locally at a specialty kitchen store, and craft stores may have a few choices.

KITCHENAID STAND MIXER

Stand mixers are found anywhere premium kitchen appliances are sold. They are very expensive, but worth it. They will last for years. If you can wait until the day-after-Thanksgiving sales (aka Black Friday), there are usually some good deals.

Gift Giving

Using your imagination for cookie-packaging ideas is almost as fun as baking the cookies.

CLEAR SIDE GUSSET BAGS

Pretzel rods and a stack of drop cookies will fit nicely in these food-safe bags. They can be found at ClearBags.com and in specialty kitchen stores. Tie with a pretty ribbon for presentation.

MASON JARS

They can be found in most local grocery stores as well as at Walmart. To decorate them, cut a square piece of fabric to place over the lid and then tie it on with a coordinating ribbon.

PLASTIC, PAPER, AND METAL HOLIDAY CONTAINERS

Dollar stores, grocery stores, and more carry Christmas-themed containers made especially for gifting Christmas cookies.

Index

Acknowledgments

I WANT TO THANK MY HUSBAND for being patient and taking care of me during the writing process. Special thanks to Loretta, my daughter, my Aunt Wanda, Ginny and Aileen for introducing me to some of their special recipes.

About the Author

Carroll Pellegrinelli, a bestselling author, has been baking for as long as she can remember. Under her mother's guidance, she began creaming butter and sugar for making cookies as soon as she could reach the counter. A few years later, her father took up bread baking. Carroll soon followed suit and began baking bread. For almost 20 years, Carroll wrote about desserts and baking for About.com. Her first book, *Travel with the Lee Girls as They Shop and Eat Their Way through the South: New Orleans and the French Quarter*, combines her love of food and travel. Her second book, *Starter Sourdough: The Step-by-Step Guide to Sourdough Starters, Baking Loaves, Baguettes, Pancakes, and More*, was a *Wall Street Journal* bestseller. Both titles are available in paperback and as e-books.

CPSIA information can be obtained
at www.ICGtesting.com
Printed in the USA
JSHW050048041220
9900JS00004B/6

9 781647 397227